T0129345

FROM
WITNESSING
TO
THRIVING

Art Therapy, Political and Religious Violence

Parisa Amirmostofian

BALBOA.
PRESS
A DIVISION OF HAY HOUSE

Balboa Press books may be ordered through booksellers or by contacting:

Balboa Press
A Division of Hay House
1663 Liberty Drive
Bloomington, IN 47403
www.balboapress.com.au
1 (877) 407-4847

Because of the dynamic nature of the Internet, any web addresses or links contained in this book may have changed since publication and may no longer be valid. The views expressed in this work are solely those of the author and do not necessarily reflect the views of the publisher, and the publisher hereby disclaims any responsibility for them.

The author of this book does not dispense medical advice or prescribe the use of any technique as a form of treatment for physical, emotional, or medical problems without the advice of a physician, either directly or indirectly. The intent of the author is only to offer information of a general nature to help you in your quest for emotional and spiritual well-being. In the event you use any of the information in this book for yourself, which is your constitutional right, the author and the publisher assume no responsibility for your actions.

Cover Design: Flame Fish Designs

Any people depicted in stock imagery provided by Getty Images are models, and such images are being used for illustrative purposes only.
Certain stock imagery © Getty Images.

Print information available on the last page.

ISBN: 978-1-5043-1957-7 (sc)
ISBN: 978-1-5043-1958-4 (e)

Balboa Press rev. date: 11/04/2019

FOREWORD

This book is written for every single human being who has been touched by trauma. It is for those of us who have lived, heard and witnessed events of cruelty that have left invisible scars, preventing us from living our most fulfilled lives. It is for everyone who has felt hallowed, haunted, or frozen by something of the past.

From Witnessing to Thriving is based on heuristic research. In some respects, it is an all-encompassing journey that entails how I healed from the PTSD I suffered from for nearly 30 years, post revolution in Iran. I have reviewed pre-existing literature on religious and political violence and war, and the effect this type of trauma has on human psychology, human rights and women's rights. I've found that witnessing cruelty causes splitting in the psyche of those who witness it. Using the art therapy method (ATTP) in combination with the heuristic methodology, helped me gain clarity about myself, as well as providing me with a new perspective and schema about the world. I no longer switch between the split selves of victim and survivor. Today, I see myself as someone who can thrive. Within these pages, I will show you how I healed and prove that you can too.

By writing this book, I am hoping to raise consciousness and highlight politics, religion and organizations that promote and push detrimental ideas and agendas. It is my deepest desire that writing this book will raise awareness around the world and relieve witnesses of the pain they were never aware of suffering from. We have all witnessed and carried pain and confusion in our psyches, often without noticing how deeply it wounds us. I'd also like to introduce a technique to free their souls of this pain. Without awareness and clarity, we wouldn't know what to do or how to heal.

*there are journal notes during processing and revisiting traumatic memories from the past included; the paintings are visual expressions related to those memories.

* client's name are pseudo-name to protect client's confidentiality.

DEDICATION

I would like to dedicate this book to all the victims and witnesses of political and religious violence, who are suffering and experiencing helplessness and hopelessness in the face of cruelty to humanity. The people who think the enemies (politics and religion) are so strong and out of reach, have no choice other than to submit.

I would like to add that the enemies (politics and religion) are ideas rooted in our own minds, and if we start clearing our minds from them, we will lead to freedom.

I also would like to dedicate this book to the field of art therapy, which has helped me believe that there is a remedy for healing broken souls.

ACKNOWLEDGMENTS

I would like to thank the people who never give up and spread love, kindness, happiness, justice and freedom. The people who follow their dreams and passions in life and keep the light on, as they pass the torch with their amazing creations. Without them, the world would have been a dark place.

CONTENTS

"Knife of cruelty has three edges, when it is in use, it cuts perpetrator, victim and witness at the same time."

PART 1
Witnessing

"It is a dark night, one more night of indwelling into my past dark childhood memories. I am alone and surrounded with paint and papers. Dark red, murky brown and black paint has stained almost everything in this room; it appears as if I am in the midst of chaos and turmoil of the revolution and war in Iran all over again.

At this point, I allowed myself to step into my long-repressed memories to take them all out and put it on the paper. I was willing to explore my deepest painful memories which have been suppressed and repressed for over 30 years. I started painting; I seized my thoughts and took the role of an observer and just observed my emotions and feelings, which flooded to surface freely. I allowed my hands to be guided by my emotions and just paint and express the experience of the moment. My right hand chose to use blue, the color of rain and water to wash the canvas, as I was unconsciously preparing the surface for the big explosion of negative emotions. I was cooling down the surface with blue anticipating the fire of rage to surface soon. After putting the blue paint on the paper, I then found the courage to draw guns, blood, dead bodies, and to display the trauma of my surroundings; the consequences of war and it's cruelty against humanity. The blue color made me feel safe enough to illustrate the dark memories that encompassed my reality. The painting, itself, seems to scream.

"Image 3, War"

Red tears slide down the blue canvas. Everyone is hurt and in a state of pain. There is a girl covering her face in fear and crying blood, for all those lost to hideous crimes. She hides her face from the bodies of innocent children, mothers and fathers. This girl is me, and the tears are mine. I have a strong desire to finish this painting. I feel as though I owe this piece of painting to the people who suffered. I need to expose these atrocities. The painting is a representation of trauma. Innocent people lie in pools of their blood and a deep river runs through the canvas, connecting us all. There is a hand above my head, spreading injustice. People have been manipulated, hypnotized, and controlled; ignorant people whose ridiculous beliefs kept them blind from the truth. They condoned the war and executions for a seat in heaven. They believed in empty promises from Islamic leaders. I watch the river of blood flow, and I tell Khomaynee and his followers to stop. The stop signs dripping with human blood are everywhere. Stop killing, stop...."

The Burden of Being a Witness

Witnessing the cruelty that accompanies political movement and war has greatly affected me. In order to shine light on the consequences of this misconstrued subject, I realized that I needed to share my story. By doing so, I wish to give voice to the pain of those who have witnessed atrocity and extreme violence. I want to convey the shock, fear and horror that witnesses feel as they watch perpetrators commit misdeeds against victims and liberate them from their pain.

In 1979, I was a 14-year-old girl living in Iran. My father was a general in royal Pahlavie's regime military. I was a voracious reader with dreams of becoming a doctor. Those dreams were shattered overnight. Like most revolutions, this political movement carried out an incredible amount of bloodshed and cruelty. After one year, the war between Iraq and Iran spread like wildfire, and the experiences addressed in this book are referring to those times of disturbance in my life.

Witnessing violence instilled fear left me with memories that created feelings of anxiety and confusion long after the initial experience had passed. I felt forced to identify with either being a victim or a perpetrator. As a victim, I'd feel emotional pain as though I experienced the cruelty within my own body. As a perpetrator, I'd feel overwhelmed with rage and revenge—I'd look for someone to blame.

Human beings cannot stay indifferent to events such as the one I experienced. Even as bystanders, we personalize things in order to understand them. Our brains automatically fire into meaning-making mode. It's our natural tendency to judge and stand in a firm position because it gives us a sense of stability. When we witness something disturbing, our memories of that experience become a part of our memory storage. Whether it's wanted or unwanted, we need to process that data.

Witnessing the cruelty of the revolution and war in Iran stole my mind for years. I couldn't enjoy the beauty in front of me. Songs I enjoyed in my youth took me back to the turmoil of the revolution. I wasn't present to life. The adolescence years are the year of identity formation. When a teenager is consumed with safety and a sense of danger, their mental and emotional development delays, or stops forever. My identity formation as a teenager was delayed. For some who witnessed the same injustice as me, their identity was foreclosed. After 30 years, I realized I needed to heal.

Politics and Religion

My decision to heal lead to a powerful revelation:

Politics and religion are the most commonly used tools for those who perpetuate violence and cruelty. That revelation brought this question to light: Why is our identity so strongly interwoven with these two notions?

When we think about politics, one of the first things that comes to mind is the dichotomy of "us vs. them". Even talking about politics creates thoughts of discrepancy and division. Whether it's discussed in the context of the country, city, or organization, politics will yield separation.

Is it because of politics that our sense of who we are is linked to a specific ideology, group, organization, and culture? Does our need to belong always impose itself upon our identity? Is who we are and what we like imposed upon us by this powerful phenomenon?

I wanted to know if we, as a human collective, could ever become truly free of social attachment and ideology? Maybe the problem is our conditionings and our sense of belonging that enforces a desire to belong to a group. Maybe our fear of abandonment is a great motivator. Part of my mission was to dig deeper.

Love and Fear

Love and fear are two prevailing life forces. We experience them holistically through our emotions, body, mind, and spirit. Every action we take stems from either love or fear. Love leads us to connect to divine values: joy, kindness, justice, creativity and freedom. Fear engenders injustice. These two life forces are on opposite spectrums from one another. They cannot coexist. It is impossible to be a fearful lover. You cannot experience divine values such as freedom or kindness while in a state of fear.

One of the most powerful tools for politicians and religions is to instill fear in mass. With the help of the media and propaganda, they manipulate and induce ideas in people's mind that make them anxious. This way controlling mass is possible.

Sense of belonging

As humans, we have a desire to be connected. We yearn to belong. It appears we feel safer when we are united with others. It makes the feeling of being small and insignificant disappear. We are connected on a spirit level, like drops of water in the ocean—we are the ocean. Yet, it is hard to distinguish drop from drop when we're looking out at a vast, majestic body of water. At the same time in this physical world, we are experiencing separation and individuality. The challenge is to remember that we are one, regardless of our experiences on this planet. We crave to establish our individuation, but within us is also a deep, hidden desire to be a part of the whole. This apparent physical separation and individuality leads to the greatest fears of all, the fear of loneliness and abandonment. This is the reason that humans are so afraid and sensitive to rejection.

Separation from the self

This fear of abandonment plays a significant role in every one's life. In fact, it starts in infancy. A fetus takes shape and becomes human inside its mother. After birth, the newborn is separated from the mother symbolically by the cutting of the umbilical cord. The real separation doesn't happen there. In a cosmic sense, a child's cord is always attached to his or her mother. No matter how old her children are, a mother always feels an intense sense of connection to her children. It is something that unites us. A newborn, however, cannot distinguish self from others, believing that the caregiver is an extension of his or her physical existence. Gradually, the child starts to realize that his mother is separate from him. She exists outside of him and must meet his needs as well as her own. Separation anxiety begins at eight months, at which point is when stranger anxiety kicks in. The little child realizes that he is on his own and that there are forces in the external world that could harm him.

Growing out of an attachment to a caregiver is intense work for a child. In this sense, the need and desire to be connected to another human being has been promoted and reinforced since childbirth, making the desire to connect and love imperative to life.

Parents have an innate desire to protect their children and to teach them the life lessons they have learned. We want to spare our children the pain we've endured. Usually, those lessons prioritize teaching a child about the dangers of life and what things to avoid. These lessons tend to be about safety and are based purely off fear. If a child behaves in certain way, his or her actions are generally judged as either good or bad. The people around them are the ones labeling their actions. Gradually, a free-spirited little kid learns to act a certain way to grab the attention of those around him. For example, if a child needs to throw a tantrum to get his parents attention, he learns to get what he wants by throwing tantrums as an adult. Conversely, if a child acts kind and sweet and is constantly praised for it, she learns to act sweet at all times, especially when she needs attention from others. Parents can and often do reinforce certain behaviors in their children by the use of reward and punishment, otherwise known as operant conditioning. This creates a construct for a child to act and think in a certain way. By extension, this tells them who to be and how to live as they age.

A Universal Need for Connection

It seems that we have not yet fully grasped or integrated how human beings operate. From the moment the umbilical cord is cut, humans lose touch with the universal truth that we are connected to all of nature. Each of us becomes a lost soul. At this moment, we crave connection to others without recognizing that we were never separated in the first place.

I felt that if I knew and better understood this problem, maybe then I could help myself and others to cultivate a more fulfilled life. I decided to use my personal experiences and dive back into my life and memories with hope that I find some solutions and ways to proceed in regards to healing the victim and the witness. I sought to explore the reasons we feel so disconnected and separate, and to discover why after all these years we continue to create war and chaos.

It is known that those who perpetrate hostility and violence are the most fearful and anxious individuals. They are so insecure and dreadful that their sense of identity is dependent on a specific ideology, ethnicity, race or culture. They perceive the existence of others as a threat to their own existence.

Many perpetrators of violent crime are sociopaths; for them hurting and killing others stems from an innate desire to create pain. These people either act alone and are thus labeled as criminals or attach themselves to a group or ideology, and in doing so find a justified way to express their subliminal desire to create pain and suffering in others. All perpetrators have one thing in common: none of them have access to the divine signature of human essence. They lack the desire for kindness, freedom, justice, love, happiness and creativity. They can be cunning and innovative when it comes to killing and hurting others, but they never have access to the divine creation of beauty. They don't know what justice is and they certainly don't understand the nature of freedom. They are prisoners of their own fears.

For those who identify with a specific culture, group, ideology or religion, this deep fear of losing identity makes them want to protect their essence. They do this by controlling and abusing others. They can easily justify taking away someone else's life and right to freedom. I noticed that the most aggressive people in my original country are those that are uneducated and misinformed. They have a primitive consciousness and low IQ's. Easily manipulated by power mongers and money, it's these ordinary civilians who are the ones to actually abuse and hurt others under the order of supreme power.

It seemed as though these people were under a spell. They would die or kill just because. What was in it for them? They received absolutely no reward of any kind; not physical, emotional, not even spiritual. The only thing these people were protecting was their sense of identity because without ideology, they were nothing.

I know the revolution of Iran wasn't due to poverty, pain or suffering. The revolution was a carefully constructed plan to dethrone a king and gain control over one of the richest countries in the world. Religion and politics made that possible.

Connecting Back to Self

During my research process, art therapy made it possible for me to revisit the inner and deepest parts of my psyche. This process helped relieve me of a constant state of emotional reactivity. I was trapped in a state of freeze and fight. My research opened space for my true human qualities to shine. This self-exploration allowed me to open doors to the light. It was conscious and deliberate, but not always logical. Art therapy helped me access the deepest levels of my unconscious. I explored step-by-step, until my fundamental insights were achieved. One of my most priceless insights is the realization that: "Knife of cruelty has three edges, when in use, it cuts perpetrator, victim and witness, at the same time."

Cruelty and The Effect on Humanity

We've all witnessed cruelty at some point in our lives. We're either traumatized directly or have been traumatized vicariously by hearing or seeing a story unfold on the screens in front of us. This is called secondary traumatization. When we witness something that we don't understand, it causes confusion and distress. It's human nature to suppress these disturbing experiences and get on with our lives. We'd rather not open Pandora's box of pain and suffering and confront our trauma head-on. Yet, despite our best efforts to suppress our emotions, we still suffer. The nature of cruelty cannot be ignored. At some point in our lives, the unresolved and unprocessed materials that we've suppressed deep in our psyches will re-emerge and catch up with us. Eventually, our memory networks will be activated, and our emotional disturbances will manifest into conflict in our relationships, including the one we have with ourselves.

There is an urgency to gain clarity about our life experiences as our experiences begin to compile upon on one another. Before we know it, there will be a chain of cause and effect reactions perpetuating disarray and disorder in our lives. The confusion and fear accompanying these reactions sets the foundation of our lives for years to come. Witnessing or directly experiencing an act of cruelty damages a person's sense of safety and trust. When this happens, a person becomes fear-oriented and unconsciously acts and lives to survive rather than thrive.

We all need to heal in order to have a joyful life, as all of us are capable of doing so. When we live only to survive, we constantly switch between two split and fragmented versions of ourselves. We become either the victim or a survivor. This happens unconsciously and so naturally that we don't even realize we are experiencing it. We do notice, however, that despite all the good things happening in our lives, we often feel consumed by exhaustion or pressure to rush through endless to-do lists. Some of us associate this malaise with unhappiness and begin to see life as unfair. We feel that our choices are imposed upon us or that we are victims of circumstances; others are responsible for our unhappiness. The switch between these two archetypes (victim and survivor) can happen simultaneously, spontaneously and so quickly that we may shift between these two identities and fluctuate between the role of victim and survivor in any given situation. For example, something happens that triggers the memory network of feeling unsafe, which leads to negative thoughts. These negative thoughts trigger an alarm response that something horrible might happen or a sense of danger to the self or the others (here the victim archetype is activated), which will be followed with negative images, then negative visceral sensations.

In this emotional state, a person's judgment and behavior is affected. He or she would behave in an inappropriate manner; perhaps becomes controlling, agitated, etcetera. This unrealistic sense of danger leads to activating the survivor from within. In this scenario, this person likely begins controlling others or the situation, which is absolutely unnecessary and unfit to the circumstances. Now this individual appears anxious, controlling, and angry.

Anything can trigger this chain of reaction; you can be at a party, on the beach, in the metro, or at work. Gradually, you only identify with the negative images in your head and/or the unnecessary interventions you feel are required to save yourself or others. As time passes, this person doesn't even realize that he or she is on autopilot, endlessly enslaved by an identity in flux. This person's psychological baseline becomes depressed or anxious and despite all the blessings in life, they don't experience appreciation or joy. Usually, he or she is judged as unappreciative and ungrateful.

A witness's psyche is like a library, the books would be comprised of loose pages floating in the air. Every time this person wanted to read a specific book, one of the floating pages belonging to another book would land on their lap instead. They'd become distracted by the information of that irrelevant page.

Safety and Security

If you are chasing happiness, peace, or joy in life, and feel you never fully experience the pure essence of being, then I can assure you that there is an unprocessed and unresolved experience buried deep in your psyche. You have a damaged sense of self. It is the self you perceive as weak and helpless, the part of you that couldn't protect or prevent wrongdoing. This has created mistrust and has affected your perception of protection and security in the world. You're not alone. It's happened to all of us and it leaves us feeling insecure. Somewhere along the way you decided that the world is not a safe place and you came to believe that you must stay in constant control or on watch. You think about the "what if's" and for the future. You prepare for the worst and come to expect it. This state of alert and alarm becomes the main cause of your anxiety and depression. You may realize that you take the happy moments of your life for granted. If you enjoy an experience not tinted with fear, it wouldn't feel authentic or real, at least not as real as the anxious moments of your life. You become conditioned to feel more alive when you are ready for the worst. Just like the old adage 'be prepared for rainy days', you prepare. The attention in your day-to-day life lands more on the negative pole of bad news and problems than positivity or creativity.

You develop a keen sense for danger and disarray. Consequently, you observe and create more negativity. Where your mind goes, your life grows. Science has shown that when a set of neurons fire together, they wire together. This means that the human brain gets used to certain stimuli, triggers and neurotransmitters. In order for our brains to keep a constant state of homeostasis and status quo, our minds look for these specific stimuli in every environment we occupy.

Like an addict, one learns to unconsciously look for bad news. We get triggered and become fearful, worried or anxious, and develop a coping strategy to calm the nerves. This coping strategy is not necessarily constructive. The individual eventually becomes distracted with day-to-day life events, and again, in order to feel alive as soon as they find some momentum or space to rest, they create or focus on another negative stimulus to bring them back to the status quo. Some of us do not even need to experience triggers from the outside world. We have mastered these negative patterns through our own thoughts, by automatically manufacturing a negative scenario in our head. This triggers our anxiety. At this stage, one learns not to trust their wants and needs, and by extension, to suppress their dreams and ambitions. The individual will resist any life event that might create a break or change in mental status. They develop a belief that despite their own goodness, there are mean and cruel powers in the world that will cast shadows over their head. If not prepared, they will be defeated by dark invisible forces.

The individual learns that in order to make sense of the disarray in the world he or she must learn to separate the self from what is bad or evil, to believe that there is an us vs. them. She learns gradually, or he comes to the conclusion that no matter how much effort he or she exerts, negative surprises should be anticipated along the way. Surprises one needs to work through at best, and at worst, survive. Gradually, these people become negative and despite all their hard work and successes, manifest only the opposite of what they desire. We begin to practice and accomplish the bad habit of self-sabotage, focusing more on the fear of failure than the fear of success. We lose trust in the possibility that life can be good.

We begin to perceive people as unstable and untrustworthy and build a shield around ourselves. This damages our authenticity and we gradually learn to wear a mask, becoming fake in an effort to survive. We feel unhappy and prefer to escape in socially acceptable ways. We follow people on social media that we perceive to have fulfilling and good lives. Our sense of connection to the world and other humans becomes more damaged, and we find ourselves lonely. With loneliness also comes the fear of abandonment. In order to avoid loneliness and abandonment, one learns to dismiss his or her true desires and becomes a people pleaser. She doesn't trust herself to be alone and he develops a sense of co-dependency and an unorganized attachment style. He or she sells their souls to shoulds and musts and sabotages their freedom in a misguided attempt to connect.

Not every negative characteristic you develop is the result of a traumatic experience endured in childhood. Sometimes just witnessing someone else's negative experience instills fear in you. We are bombarded with images of conflict, chaos, and war on a consistent basis. We are witness to an incredible amount of helplessness and hopelessness that many victims experience from every corner of the world. It often seems there is no end or solution in sight.

Just witnessing cruelty inflicted on another human being can damage your sense of trust and safety. Even in the event that you identify with the perpetrator and justify the situation by viewing the victim as at fault or deserving of punishment, witnessing the pain inflicted on a victim, whether physical or emotional, triggers your innate sense of empathy and compassion. Many people suppress this reaction because they believe they aren't supposed to show compassion to an enemy. This causes confusion in the witness and creates unresolved emotional reactivity. At some point, that negatively impacts the witnesses' psyche and corrupt their energy field.

Our first emotional reaction when witnessing cruelty is a mixed bag of emotions: empathy, sympathy, compassion, and confusion. In order to make sense of those emotions we judge. We run the situation through our heads and because cruelty is impossible to reconcile, our thoughts lead us to a secondary set of emotions that often include anger, sadness and blame. In a better sense we emotionally react to our initial emotional reaction.

As an example, when people who call themselves Muslims or identify as being religious gather to watch a woman being stoned, they contribute to the collective agreement that the woman is sinful, worthy of being tortured to death. They judge the act of stoning to be a holy and godly act. They rationalize this act of cruelty with religious and political justifications. In reality, witnessing this act of cruelty, seeing the victim in pain, triggers an innate sense of empathy and sympathy. Witnesses attempt to suppress this feeling because they have no choice but to dehumanize the victim and judge her as being sinful and dirty. They manipulate themselves into being angry with the victim for creating such a negative spectacle. Their rage and anger can actually lead them to grab stones and throw them at the victim themselves. While acting cruel, they actually have mixed emotions and are conflicted, struggling with a deep sense of empathy, fear, and rage. Understanding our capacity to experience compassion and empathy requires us to clarify our stance on humanity. We must come to know ourselves better.

Human's Blue Print

As humans, our emotional experiences are perceived holistically. We experience them through our physical body, thoughts, mental images, and emotions. When triggered by an act of cruelty, our thoughts tend to follow a specific trajectory of emotion, while our rational mind makes meaning out of the situation. We judge the situation and discern whether or not what is unfolding is appropriate and assign a certain level of acceptability. Your mind starts anticipating and predicting next step scenarios, what might, could, or should happen. It seems that humans can't just experience life on an instinctual level free of judgment. There are individuals who can experience emotion without assigning thoughts to it, reaching that level of awareness requires a certain kind of wisdom and a highly evolved conscious. This is achievable for everyone, but the first step to building awareness is developing a greater understanding for compassion, empathy, and sympathy, knowing that they are innate and natural to human beings.

It is interesting to see how these authentic forms of emotions are confusing to people. There are so many books, talks and teachings about compassion. But in this current cycle of political chaos, global warming and the general feeling of malaise, division, and confusion, it seems that compassion is gradually fading away from the collective human conscience. Some of us have even had learned to resist compassion and view it as a limitation.

When people develop mistrust and are consumed with fear for safety and security, they have a hard time feeling or expressing compassion. Rather than being attentive to their feelings or the feelings of others, they rationalize and question other's motives when they are experiencing fear or pain.

Sympathy and Empathy

We experience sympathy when we hear a story about someone and judge that story as sad. We feel sorry for a person who suffers or is in a state of pain. We wish better for them. Ultimately, sympathy is only an acknowledgment of pain in others from afar.

Empathy and compassion differ in both subtle and significant ways from sympathy. Empathy is triggered naturally and unconsciously disregard of our judgment about the story. But in order to elicit sympathy, we need a story and to derive meaning from that story, we need to justify the situation as bad or good, without our judgment sympathy is not possible.

Compassion

What is Compassion? Is it the capacity to see clearly into the nature of suffering?

Compassion is the moment we realize that we are not separate from others.

Compassion has an essential component that can't be merged with the rational mind. Compassion doesn't require justification. It is an inherent human quality, but in order for compassion to be freely expressed, we've learned that certain conditions need to be attached to the person or situation we can feel it for.

Our rational mind has so much control over our ability to be compassionate. At times, we suppress it due to fear, insecurity, or simply because we can't relate to the person or situation. We can easily suppress compassion with logical reasoning. As Joan Halifax says, compassion has many enemies and some of them are pity, moral outrage, and fear. Our society is paralyzed by fear and that fear is global. In part we feel this fear because of a deep-seated insecurity.

As an example, we are taught to not feel compassionate for our enemies. We think they deserve what they get. Our ideologies tend to surpass and diminish our innate sense of compassion. If we have experienced a painful situation in the past, we become more sensitive when we see someone else is experiencing it, we even experience it vicariously to a certain extent.

Viewing a person in pain and sadness is enough to spark compassion. We are made of energy and bio-photons, and we have an energy field around our bodies. This energy field responds to our thoughts and emotions. Dr. Rupert Sheldrake biologist who has researched cell biology and consciousness, names our energy field as Morphic field, which generates our behavioral, biological, social and mental activities. Morphic field is common among every single organism and humans, it is the storage of memory, and human's connections to universe and to one another.

When we experience pain or fear, the frequency of our energy field vibration changes. The energy field of our brain resonates with the energy field of planet earth. This is known as Schumann resonance. When there are disturbances in this energy field it effects whoever is in touch with it. This is especially apparent in relationships with those with whom we are close. We are prone to the changes in energy of the people that we feel emotionally connected to, disregard of physical distance. Depression, anxiety, and happiness are contagious. Without verbal communication, we feel other people's emotional state. This is known as empathy. We feel empathy through our body and emotions. We feel it in our physical, mental, and emotional planes.

The difference between compassion and empathy is that empathy is when you feel another person's feeling, and you become one with the other person's suffering. Empathic person lacks the ability to separate self from the other person's pain. It appears as flu virus that can travel from one person to another and make them both equally sick.

Compassion is empathy in action and studies have shown that it reduces anxiety and depression and decreases bias towards others as well as emotional tension. Compassion is the ability to feel the level of person's suffering and finding a way to meet fundamental humanly needs for the other person. It is possible through affection and connection to another human being, which results to compelling sense of belonging, being heard and felt. A compassionate individual has ears for call of help and shares empathy and offer comfort.

Compassion accompany sense of responsibility for making another person feel better. Studies have shown that making the sufferer feel better will make the witness feel better. A compassionate person is more resilient when it comes to witnessing the suffering of others.

Kindness

Kind people are compassionate because they feel secure. They are self-reliant and confident. They trust themselves to handle pain and believe in the beauty of life and nature. Kind people have no fear of allowing themselves and others experience the full range of emotions. They are secure emotional beings and they are not scared of being vulnerable. They are aware of the nature of vulnerability and realize they need to take action when empathy arises within them. Kind people tend toward empathy and compassion rather than sympathy. They take responsibility for the energy of sorrow when it is activated within them. Kind people experience life to the fullest and demonstrate a certain degree of resiliency and strength. Kind people are generous in heart and mind and that allows them to experience freedom. They become successful in any endeavor they take on in life because they are strong- hearted and courageous. They carry a great level of bravery and trust in their own actions. They are men and women of faith, not religious faith but faith in humanity. They make great friends, parents, and children. People love them dearly. Kind people are proactive and don't suffer from anxiety or depression. We have to differentiate kind people from people pleasers; people pleasers are those who make kind gestures and take action out of fear. People pleasers are co-dependent and experience high levels of anxiety. As a result, they become pushovers and continuously look for acknowledgment and appreciation. Their sense of inadequacy and insecurity pushes them to act kindly only to get closer to others. They have learned that when they are kind, other people let them in more easily. Contrarily, an authentically kind person acts from a secure and stable place, not out of need or weakness. Kind people are not looking for rewards or payback. Acts of kindness shower the brain with Gaba and Serotonin neurotransmitters, creating sensations of joy and peace.

Kindness is one of the divine virtues, alongside happiness, love, freedom, and justice. Divine values are different cuts and faces of the same diamond. Every angle shows the majestic beauty of the whole diamond. An act of kindness is innate and deeply rooted in our soul. It is not teachable. We experience it through our heart chakra. Kind and resilient people feel a certain level of freedom when it comes to experiencing compassion. They are more prone and sensitive to experience in general. At the same time, they can return to their natural baseline faster than uncompassionate people.

Individuals who suppress compassion due to fear or rationalization become depressed, agitated, and angry. When one suppresses compassion, they also suppress a certain level of freedom for themselves. This limitation blocks the energy of other forms of amazing feelings like love and kindness. People will suppress compassion to protect themselves from getting hurt.

They don't trust their strength and ability to be resilient and instead choose to keep the door closed to floods of unbearable emotions. People who lack compassion have difficulty connecting to others and life. These people are locked in prisons of fear, with the key to freedom lost somewhere within their unconscious mind.

We are exposed to psychosocial and spiritual toxins every day. These toxins leak from fear and our lack of clarity about who we are and what to believe in this time of political chaos and confusion. When we separate ourselves from the whole humanity and life and instead, try to control our natural, innate expression of emotion, we lose our authenticity. In doing so, we betray ourselves and lose trust and respect for everything, including ourselves. This sense of distrust damages our self-esteem. As a result, we end up with low self-confidence. No matter how high our social status or the amount of money in our bank account, still, we are suffering.

The reason we fear compassion is because we have the capacity to feel it for anybody, with no boundaries, regardless of social status, religion, ideology, and ethnicity. Compassion brings us closer to everyone, and in response to that sensation, we feel exposed. To be compassionate, we have to let go of our identity and social status. We have to bring down the shield of me vs. you, us vs. them. We have to become one with life with no exclusion. For some, this exposure is too much, and they can't handle it. It is important to know that compassion doesn't make us vulnerable; it makes us strong as a person and nation.

Compassion gives us the capacity to be open to the world and to have an open and free heart. The biggest fear an uncompassionate person has is the arrival of pain and sorrow in others. It evokes an inner and deep pain that they are scared to face. At a very young age, these people learned to suppress their pain because the adults around them were unable to acknowledge and respect it. Their caregivers taught them life lessons instead of divine virtues. When kids suffer, some parents react anxiously. They seek to solve the problem for their children and in the process, oppress the sorrow and emotions of their children and attempt to use the experience as an opportunity to teach life lessons. Rather than providing their children with a safe and trusting emotional space that would allow them to experience pain and growth, these parents get angry with their kids. They perceive the expression of negative emotions as weakness. These children eventually learn to distill their feelings into anger. When they are sad, they act mad and grow into irritable and controlling individuals.

It's important to not confuse compassion with pity. Feeling pity for others comes from an unrealistic state of mind. When we regard someone with pity we perceive the individual as incapable. We see them as weak and separate from others without realizing that we are from the same essence of spirit. All of humanity comes from the same source. We experience and express the same emotions through different stories. In essence, we wear the same suit in different shades of color.

When we feel compassion, it is impossible to separate self from others. We feel another person's pain without fear because we know we have the power to bring upon change for the suffering person. We know we are human, vulnerable and at the same time resilient, and strong. We are aware of our innate ability to create happiness and experience joy and believe that everyone can experience positive and negative emotions. We have respect for the suffering person and their suffering.

Feeling pity for others addresses a false sense of superiority within us. It is a complete illusion that separates us from life. When we believe other people to be victims, we perceive them as incapable and weak. Inevitably, we apply the same logic upon ourselves and as a byproduct, experience self-pity. This robs us of our internal resources, and we lose strength in the face of life's challenges. We only feel pity for a person who is doomed, someone with little chance of positive outcome. Pity is condescending and people react negatively when they believe they are being commiserated upon. No one wants to be weak. Weakness leads to helplessness and hopelessness.

Gradually, people who are pitied learn to be uncompassionate. They lose the sensitivity to express kindness and care. They become isolated as their sense of emotional connection diminishes. People with false sense of superiority who separate themselves from others, They gradually lean toward hedonistic behavior, grandiosity, and in extreme cases, a narcissistic personality disorder. This personality disorder fits the profile of politicians and men who see themselves as men of gods. They will reinforce the lack of empathy in our governments, abuse their power positions, and oppress human rights.

As long as we see ourselves as separate from others through race, ethnicity, and religion, we will continue to diminish our sensitivity, compassion, and ability to celebrate humanity. There is no dichotomy that truly separates us, but when we witness extreme violence and fail to take responsibility or action to bring change, we suffer incredible pain and division as a community. The vibration of the negative situation will bring the vibration of the witness down, too.

The ache that we feel in our souls feels like empathy and compassion. Don't take it lightly when you feel empathy and compassion. Those feelings are a call from your soul to help raise the universal vibration. We are all victims if we don't take charge and to create positive change.

Coping strategies and Defense Mechanism

When we face a painful situation or witness cruelty, we unintentionally employ specific defense mechanisms to make the experience tolerable. There are different defense mechanisms, such as justification, replacement, denial, repression, suppression, sublimation, reaction formation, projection and regression. Some cultures consider denial as blessing. It is one of our most primitive defense mechanisms for coping with traumatic and stressful situations. Denial starts in early childhood at the moment we begin to unconsciously deny emotions associated with a negative situation. We ignore its adverse effects on us to the point that we hardly acknowledge there is a problem. Another defense mechanism we often employ is dissociation, which is the action of disconnecting or detaching oneself from a traumatizing situation or event. This separation is related to mental processes and results in one group of neurons functioning independently from the rest. The person facing the traumatic experience moves through the situation in a state of shock and acts or reacts without grasping the extent of unfolding devastation. Their emotions are turned off. In extreme cases this leads to disorders such as Dissociative Identity Disorder, otherwise known as multiple personality disorder

These mental and safety reactions will help build up tolerance for the person experiencing the traumatizing situation in a way that prevents them from breaking to pieces. Dissociation preserves and freezes our mental functioning in order to help us cope until the negative situation passes. It prevents emotional devastation.

The problem with denial and dissociation is that the shock will stay in your mental and nervous system and cause disturbances in your life. At some point people develop PTSD (Post traumatic stress Disorder). There is no way to forgive and forget if you have not processed the experience that caused your trauma; you cannot rationalize the situation or accept it as it is.

In order to accept an act of cruelty on another human and be ok with it, you need to be a sociopath. Therefore, you can't cope with witnessing brutality if it happens at your presence. Witnessing cruelty has an unequivocally damaging effect on your mental and emotional wellbeing. I have clients who have not experienced a traumatic event in real life but have watched a fictitious movie convincing enough to traumatize them. Ironically, you don't have to suffer traumatic events directly to experience psychological turmoil. You can experience confusion just by witnessing a traumatic event.

Jenny (pseudo-name) was a 24-year-old client who didn't trust men. She couldn't start an intimate relationship at the time we began our work. Despite her beauty and charm, once a romance evolved toward intimacy, she would end the relationship. It's important to note that Jenny never endured a traumatizing experience with a member of the opposite sex. She had a loving family and a good relationship with her father. After assessing her case, she was able to unfold the origin of her mistrust for male figures. As we delved into her fear, she remembered watching a movie that showed a rape scene during her adolescence. Just as her body was changing into that of a woman and during the time of sexual identity formation, the scene stuck and significantly affected her. It reinforced a narrative that told her to distrust men with physical intimacy. The fear she experienced while watching the rape scene buried itself deeply in her unconscious. Once Jenny realized her problems stemmed from watching a movie she was able to overcome her fear of physical intimacy. She was surprised to realize how vulnerable and sensitive the human mind is. This is not to say that humans are not remarkably resilient. Trauma impacts us all differently, but we are also sensitive, and the consequences of trauma can vary depending on how and when the exposure initially occurred.

Those that demonstrate immediate resiliency in the face of trauma are still emotionally affected by the event. They simply have better coping skills, defense mechanisms and more social support. They can take care of themselves, but for those that don't have the same coping skills trauma hurts to the core.

We intend to suppress and repress our unresolved issues which we feel we have no resolution or strength to face them. In order we gather our strength to face life despite it's atrocity and difficulties we need to use our defense mechanism, this is the only way our ego can survive and move forward. But we should be aware that our defense mechanisms need to be reviewed and be replaced by more constructive coping strategies. Defense mechanisms are unconscious and have side effects, since it is like a pain killer which doesn't cure the illness but ease off the symptoms until the cure arrives. Applying coping mechanism is unconscious and it helps the individual to push through difficulty and reach to cure and resolution.

Archetypes

Human have a very complex psyche. In order to understand the complexity of how we function mentally scholars such as Freud and Jung classified and categorized human's psyche to different levels with certain functioning assigned to it. One of the magnificent findings is that human functions in conscious and unconscious level, which these activities are practically making the one's life. Carl Jung the 20th century psychiatrist and founder of analytical psychology suggests that human psyche has a profound structure which is called unconscious and influences how we experience the world. Jung says there exist identical psychic structures common to all, which are heritable and influence the way we all humans experience the world. Jung calls these structures archetypes, these archetypes influence our lives, they are related to symbols, human's identity and religious and cultural experiences and rituals. Archetypes have influence on human's thoughts and behaviors that gives right to similarities among human disregard of their ethnicity race or religious background.

Psyche is made of conscious, personal unconscious and collective unconscious. These three realms are not separated from one another, they interact. The conscious mind is the field of awareness which the person has knowledge of. The unconscious is the realm that stores psychic contents which one is unaware of and is divided to two different parts. The personal unconscious and the collective unconscious. The personal unconscious is particular to each individual, it consists of life event that are either insignificant or forgotten or are repressed due to their disturbing and stressful nature. There is a deeper and more fundamental unconscious which is called by Jung as collective unconscious. The collective unconscious consists of psychic structures or cognitive categories, which are not unique to the individual but rather shared by all, influencing our thoughts and behavior. The collective unconscious is home to archetypes. "from the unconscious there emanates determining influences, which independently of tradition, guarantee in every single individual a similarity and even a sameness of experience."

We have no awareness of our archetypes in action. A healthy mind relies on the healthy functioning of its archetypes. In order to notice the existence of our archetypes is through the manifestation of symbolic imagery, it is only through interpretation of symbols who come to our conscious through dreams and visual expressions, mythology and so forth. These symbolic and imagery expressions is not the same for each person rather they are shaped and deeply connected to the persons beliefs, religious and cultures. The development of archetypes is the results of common shared millions of years of human development. By becoming increasingly aware of archetypal patterns and the symbols that they manifest in our psyche we experience expansion of our consciousness. The evolutions of consciousness is the ultimate purpose for human.

The known and common archetypes are; the Self, The Innocent, The Orphan, The Warrior Hero, The Caregiver or Great Mother, The Seeker, The Lover, The Rebel, The Creator, The Ruler, The Magician, The Sage or the Wise man, The Joker Jester.

Jung, states that the symbolic images made by individuals are a mixture of personal and archetypal part of the psyche. He valued the interpretation of arts by the patients that could bring about synthesis of personal and archetypal material. The collective unconscious expresses itself through the personal unconscious. Jung further asserts that the personal unconscious is complex, and the collective unconscious is structured by the archetypes. Jung gives special attention to the meaning that the patient put on the images which the meaning can be integrated into life. The archetypes are in the deep levels of the individual's unconscious and can stay unrevealed until activated by events in person's life experiences.

During this research project I found two essential and important archetypes which come to manifestation in here and now when a person is facing life challenges and cruelty. These two archetypes are; The Victim, and The Survivor. During my art therapy research at illumination phase, the two dominant symbols which kept presenting itself as a pair through different imagery and symbols were The Victim and The Survivor. In forward pages we will explore and discuss these two archetypes and their roles in our psyche especially when we are witnessing the cruelty.

Our Shadow

We tend to burry our dark and negative traumatic experiences deep into our unconscious. One of the most fascinating aspect in our unconscious mind is our shadow, which has been introduced by Jung, apparently our shadow is deep and dark compromised of our deep-rooted unacceptable desires and negative ideas and fears. We use and apply our defense mechanism to allow these unacceptable desires to surface and to be experienced. For example, if a person has pedophile desires but is aware of this dark and sinful and unacceptable act, will unconsciously use sublimation defense mechanism, and will find a legal and socially acceptable way to be around children such as becoming a pre-school teacher. This person's dark desire is buried in his shadow and he is unaware of its presence. But at some point, in life this dark and malice desire might come to surface and make the person to take the first criminal act.

Or when an individual enjoys causing pain and hurt to others and this desire is deep buried in their unconscious and buried in their shadow, they unconsciously use defense mechanism sublimation and this desire will manifest into more sociably acceptable job such as a police officer. These individuals unconsciously will use brutality in their job force and can cross boundaries. Also there are other form of defense mechanisms which are used to help the dark desires from the shadow to come to surface and manifest into actions. For example if a man has homosexual desire and culturally he labels them as bad or sinful, they feel so much unconscious aggression and anger toward those internal desires, these individual will develop an unconscious self-hate, and when they face a homosexual person they use reaction formation as defense mechanism and they act extremely aggressive against LGBY people, they will become extremists who are willing to bit and torture homosexuals.

There are so many people in political parties, police enforcement, military and organizations, churches and house of Gods and schools who are using their jobs as cover up for their deep dark desires from their shadows to hurt people, and these individuals are the ones who bring brutality and injustice to their systems and hurt people to the core.

Knowing our shadows and trying to help self and others to become aware of their deep dark desires rather than unconsciously reacting to them will lead us all to health and freedom.

Maya, Matrix, and Creativity;

Our physical life experiences is our reality, which according to ancient wisdom is Maya and in western civilization is known as Matrix. The reality is designed for our spirits to experience creativity and re-experience the divine source of creation. We are embodying different dimensions in life through our consciousness, in this quest we are guided with our emotions experiencing contrast and making choices. Practically it is our emotions that gives color to life and is the background music during the experiences that we endeavor. The only thing can allow us to experience the divine source is through our creativity. Creativity is our divine signature. We breath, we love, we laugh, we go through the rainbow of emotions. The supreme feeling and emotion is love, which is unexplainable, untouchable, strong and soft and tender. When it comes to love we become free, it seems it just moves softly and swiftly covers everything absolutely everything in our internal world, love creates happiness, joy, kindness, beauty, justice and freedom.

Due to our immense connection in energy level, we feel all creation and every single play of characters on this planet, we carry unlimited form and shapes of archetypes, any roles, any energy that has ever been created on this planet, we are part of a whole, we all move together. As a collective conscious we all go through ups and downs together, we have ear for any sound that has ever been created in this universe, we have eyes to see any possible creations in this world, we have tenderness to feel with our energy field and our heart. We are so deeply connected to the point that we have unlimited access to all. It appears our psyche has layers and when we pass the ego filter, we ascertain entry to Akashik record, to collective morphogenic field. Our consciousness is expanding with the expansion of universe, our universe is becoming vaster and more beautiful and we are part of this amazing movement and growth. The all is this ocean of energy and every single drop carries the majestic and miraculous transcript of the whole.

We experience the whole history of this universe through our emotions and feelings. That is why when we look at a small beautiful flower grown in the crack of concrete drive way it grabs our attention and we experience life just by looking at this little fragile thing. A child's smile connects us to the universal experience of beauty, love, birth, happiness and innocence of life. We need to wake up and acknowledge that we know, that we are aware, and we are part of whole.

Still in our abysmal deep dark shadow we have all kind of repressed ideas, weaknesses, fears, creatures who are formed as criminals, whom we kept them prisoners and don't allow them to come to surface, every single creature carries certain characteristics which with every single movement creates a wave of different energies, we learn not to allow their negative energy creates disturbances in our shared universal consciousness, we learn to be part of this amazing body of light vibration. We need to make waves with love, to make waves with beauty, to make waves with kindness, to make waves with joy, we learn freedom of soft and majestic movement of the whole.

We have different archetypes in our unconscious, it is up to us to get to know them and grant the ultimate permission of their expression. The only way to learn what do we have in our shadow is through looking at outside world, since they are projected on other people that we meet in our lives. We meet people who we idealize as heroes, we see people who are a representation of love and beauty, we witness the expression of greed and cruelty. When we notice certain characteristic and we immediately judge them as good or bad is due to our knowledge of their nature, because they are representing different aspects of ourselves. They are helping us to have a glance into our own shadow. Of course, when we meet one negative aspect from our shadow projected to outside world, we immediately resent it, we don't want to face the ugly nature of our fears, that makes us frightened, angry, and stressed, we won't like what we saw.

If we bear in mind that the things, we don't like in outside world are projected aspects of our internal world, then we learn to acknowledge the responsibility to heal ourselves and save the world, we will take responsibility to bring upon positive changes. If we see cruelty and darkness, we should increase light and love and kindness. If we close our eyes on what is before us and don't claim any responsibility and as a witness separate ourselves from what we see, we lose connection to the source right then and there, this disconnection on Tree of Life is called Abyss, It is losing touch with the whole and as the result we experienc life in a void. If we turn our head and do nothing we have abetted in its commission. Seeing a child in poverty and doing nothing increases the energy of ignorance, neglect, and down fall of human's energy field.

When we witness cruelty before our eyes, we experience the existence of victim, perpetrator and witness, in a better sense we become all three. every person involved in that situation is representation of different aspects of our deep-rooted personalities, archetype of victim and archetype of perpetrator. Allowing the perpetrators to butcher life makes us one with them. Our perpetrator in our shadow takes charge and will make a victim of us. It is us against us, it is me against me, it is personal.

The two strong archetypes who wake up in the face of witnessing cruelty are archetype of victim and archetype of perpetrator. They both are going to breath and live and takeover our life until we get to the processing and reprocessing of what we witnessed and do something about it. Negativity and darkness can only be combated with light, and love. Becoming aware of the adverse effects of witnessing cruelty on our mental and emotional wellbeing, will lead to our active participation to create change.

The reasons we didn't take action in the past was for one we thought what is going on is not our business and doesn't concern us, second we find ourselves insignificant in scale of me vs outside world. We don't realize that by taking action we are not trying to fix what is going on in outside world, we are turning the light on to combat the darkness of inside, then as collective little candles the outside world will be illuminated.

It is extremely vital and important to learn that we are responsible for our inner world, and our actions to light up our inner psyche will result to collective majestic enormous sun that will light up the whole world.

PART 2
How Did I Come About

You have heard this before; we go through certain phases and experiences in life that makes us believe it is about time, to travel back in time and address undeniable dark memories from our past. We feel the urgency to work on that specific memory since we become convinced the lost key to the door of happiness, is trapped somewhere in the dark dungeon of our unconscious mind. Finding the right path to memory is not straight forward. We usually get lost along the way. Over the years we have employed specific unconscious defense mechanisms that they kick in as soon as something triggers that particular memory network, then we get lost, overwhelmed with emotions and race of thoughts which takes us always to a dead end.

I reached to a point in my life that I had everything that I wanted. I finally settled to who I was and what I wanted to be and found my place and role. I finally felt like my ship has sailed and now is the time of discovering the amazing land that I stepped on, but there was something missing, or in a better sense there was something out of place, and that was my sense of unsettled being, I felt a sense of belonging and not belonging at the same time. I was finally at home but the place was not familiar. I had my own family, but I was afraid of losing them, I had found the love of my life and married to him, but still, I was looking for my missing half. Everything was quite perfect and complete, but I was not content. I even was consumed with safety and security; I would spend most of my time to search and study online to learn so much about secret affairs and systems underneath the calm appearance of the world. I gathered so much knowledge about secret societies, all things that governments don't want us to know, and I kept digging into darkens and exploring the dark underground affairs of the world for no apparent reason.

After I started studying psychotherapy and art therapy and going through all the self-exploration and education, I came to the conclusion that there is a dark side of my history living in Iran after revolution, which is left unprocessed and untouched, that memory was fully charged and alive but in the cage suppressed and repressed somewhere in my psyche. I got to realize that my resentment in talking about Iran or listening to Iranian music was due to these unprocessed difficult experiences that I endured living in the Islamic Republic government of Iran.

I decided to do my thesis research paper on myself and delve into the old memories of Iran; I was a whiteness to cruelty on humanity. I decided to conduct heuristic research and art therapy to access possibly to all the unresolved memories and process them one by one. I remember when I shared my plan with my teachers, they warned me of that might be tough, but I didn't care, I knew in order to step on the ground of freedom I have to free myself from the past unresolved old memories, which were chained to my feet and keeping me as slave.

I knew having access in conscious level to all the memories might not be possible since I tried that in talk therapy with my therapist and that didn't help, at some point, I even felt that I was traumatizing my therapist. I knew if I use bilateral brain stimulation, the process will be facilitated; I was ready to delve and dwell and explore and free myself.

I did use a research project that was an introspective heuristic study into my memories of political violence, religious violence, and complex trauma which resulted from exposure to war and suppression of human rights and women's rights. For me, the experience happened from early adolescence to adulthood ages 14-27 (the period of individuation and identity formation). My research study focuses on processing the effects of primary and secondary traumatization as a result of exposure to cruelty on humanity by religious violence and political violence on children and adolescents mitigated by the lack of appropriate defense mechanism and support at the time of the exposure.

During the age of 14-27, I witnessed cruelty on humans and horrific experiences in Iran. The complex traumatic experiences occurred after the

Islamic revolution and war and living under the oppressive fundamentalist's Islamic regime of Iran.

Parts of this books is referring to research and studies conducted by scholars and psychologists whom I have mentioned their name on the list of references at the end of the book, and the other part is my experience of self -exploration into traumatic memories, and my healing journey from victim/witness to a thriving soul.

The Significance of This Study

I explored the utilization of the ATTP in art therapy modality as a supportive guide on the path to discovering the effect of the exposure to political violence and religious violence resulting in symptoms of complex trauma. I also explored into a possible resolution for replacing the old dysfunctional coping skills and defense mechanisms with new coping strategies that are constructive for living after cessation of the trauma, to transform the unprocessed flight/fight and freeze responds to the more productive psychic energy. To do that I focused on the resolution of trauma symptoms through the integration of the experienced trauma and the exploration of unproductive coping skills.

This research contributes to the psychological community's understanding of exposure to cruelty on humans and the horror of war and act of religion, which can have long life consequences. The methodology of this study can be applied to discovering unresolved emotional reactions and feeling to witnessing an act of cruelty such as exposure to any crimes and violence by humans not necessarily through politic or religion motivations. I hope that this self-exploration inspires dialogue on using the power of art therapy, where it applies, to the social ills of the world. During exposure to the act of cruelty, the psychological scars and wounds will remain untouched and unprocessed since the dominant priorities are maintaining physical safety.

PART 3
Integral part of War, Violence, Masculine and Feminine Energy

A brief history of Iran during years of 1979-1992

The period that I lived in Iran: The downfall of the Pahlavi Royal regime of Iran happened in year 1979, the Islamic government that replaced it, created over 40 years of horrific human rights abuses and executions inside the country, and state-sponsored assassinations of political dissidents abroad. Women were singled out as symbols of decadence and consumerism under the Islamic government, were to bear the impact of subsequent social and gender restructuring. In brief, the fundamentalist Islamic Republic of Iran set draconian policies and the discriminatory rules against women. Indeed, women had to fight their way up in social injustice to protect their human rights, if they ever are successful.

The rules are held very rigidly by men based on essential gender attributes. Rules in Islamic fundamentalist are a gender-based hierarchy of social responsibilities and rights. Women and girls from age 9 are considered as sexualized beings capable of causing chaos and confusion in the male society if not sufficiently controlled. The Islamic regime of Iran decided for Iranian to insert religious ideas with social justice; they chose to cover women (Hijab) from head to toe, only face and hands from wrists would be exposed. The veil (Hijab) and separation are found to be necessary to prevent the dangers of female sexuality and to maintain social order and harmony.

The convergence of women and religion in Islamic fundamentalist ideology is a deliberate manipulation designed to promote the attainment and retention of political authority: The institutionalization of male interests and the subordination of women are not to be seen or understood as irrational fundamentalist policies but as carefully studied strategies grounded in politics and the hunger for power. The notion of control, and particularly the control of women, is central here.

Principle of Gender and Religion

In ancient wisdom (Hermetic) which goes back to 6500 years ago before any religion was born. One of the principles is the principle of Gender. The Principle of Gender embodies the truth that there is gender manifested in everything that masculine and feminine energy are ever present and active in all phases of phenomena, in each plane of life, physical, mental and spiritual. All the religions are derived from these principles but with lots of twists to make these wisdoms hidden as a secret from the public. Knowledge of these principles and universal laws will give men in power enough tools to manipulate people and throw them off balance and control societies. A balance society is a society who embrace and respect both genders. Respecting the equal rights of males and female will liberate, strengthen people in those societies. These people would not become slaves and won't be manipulated to war, they require equilibrium in their country, and their governments can't abuse them.

The word "Gender" is derived from the Latin root meaning to generate, to create, to produce. It has a broader meaning than sex. Sex is the physical manifestation of gender in the physical plane. We find a distinct expression of gender in micro and macro scheme of life and creation. In all establishments such as molecules, elements, plants, animals and human, the principle of gender exists and is the reason for reproduction and the existence of life. Female and male energy is needed to be balanced in a human's inner and outer world. every single human is made of masculine and feminine energy united. After provoking fear in a human's mind, individuals lose touch with their internal strengths and resources. They perceive life as an entity and affairs outside them and feel they are disconnected from the world; they view themselves separate from life and other people. Religions were successful in cutting humans off from the source of creation stemmed from inside and took the role as middlemen and agents to connect them to a fictional god, which only serve men of God's interests. Gender has lost its true meaning and equilibrium and intentionally has been promoted as sexual attires by religions. Oppression of female energy and developing a false sense of superiority in male society creates confusion and imbalance in both genders.

One of the main tasks in Islam is putting so much shame on women's body and crushing feminine energy. Feminine energy is responsible for intuition, connection with spirituality, and is the receiver of spiritual and empowering messages; feminine energy is responsible for human's divine secret which is creativity. When in society feminine energy is suppressed, it will result in the suppression of creativity and intuition in those societies. Suppression of feminine energy will lead to confusion and mental and physical poverty. In those societies crime, addiction, violence, and prostitution will increase. In such societies, people become fear oriented and can be easily manipulated and controlled by the government, and since they are tagging along with religion or ideology, their sense of identity get threatened by people from other beliefs. Liberating these people from their entangled beliefs and leaders' influence is essential to promote peace. In these societies the governments are dictators, and they all abuse their power, and they steal from people and keep the mass in poverty. The false religious beliefs blind people from the truth and cut them from their inner wisdom, they can quickly become manipulated, and they turn to slaves to work and feed the monsters in power.

In all religions there are restrict rules about gender and sexuality, especially in Islam gender segregation plays a massive role. Based on Islamic laws some traditions and customs separate men from women in social settings. The Islamic rules vary from country to country; there are diverging opinions among experts in Islamic theology which it can go to the far end of death warrant in the form of fatwa against those who allow the mixing of sexes. There is not a clear line or boundaries where the Islamic law stop. Islamic laws have been used to meet the agenda of oppression of women's right including killing, torture, rape, and stoning. The Islamic leaders have a goal in mind to disturb the equilibrium and balance in mass consciousness; they promote shame, guilt, and fear, which is the notion of most organized religions. Majority of muslim men have dogmatic beliefs about gender role, and they believe women belong at home and they supposed to take care of the family's physical needs, a girl is regarded as sinful and weak. Physical and sexual abuse is widespread in those societies and men to view women as sexual objects which have been created to sexually satisfy men and look after them, in Islamic societies women have 1/2 of men legal rights.

In the other hand, Islam promotes a false sense of superiority in men which is also dangerous for the men's psychological wellbeing.

In Islam, the main goal is to create confusion and fear in mass. oppression of women will result in male confusion. when a man doesn't respect his mother or sister or wife and view them as weak, or unworthy, that man loses his connection to his feminine energy.

In our world Women have an essential role in shaping the society; women are the mothers who bear children and are nurturers and nourishers of the whole society. Societies who embrace women power and raise liberated children are the strongest and healthiest societies. Their children won't be adults who easily manipulated or controlled, which is going to be very difficult for governments and organizations who need human resources and followers to push their agendas. The organizations are operating on slavery and manpower, without followers they can't accomplish their goals and will lose their powers. An anxious or depressed mother or a woman who is fear, shame or guilt oriented robs the society at large from their intuitive and creative influences. As a troubled mother will raise men who are imbalance with confused sense of self, these men need anchor and are lacking a sense of balance and stability. Therefore, they identify with an organization or religion or an ideology or a job to emotionally or mentally survive.

Confusion in children prepares them for slavery, they can be easily manipulated by governments and organizations. If you want to heal a society you can start with women in that society, respect and highly value them, you will be amazed by the remarkable results. When a child lives in an environment who witnesses an exchange of connection, respect, trust and love between her parents, or male and female in his society, this child's first task of connecting to their inner balance and wisdom is accomplished. The mental and emotional state of the parents does affect the mental-emotional wellbeing of the child. Studies have shown our emotional states is contagious, MRI brain studies have shown that humans unconsciously are communicating via their right brains. That means we share our emotional states, an anxious person or a depressed person can make the other person anxious and depressed, such as catching viruses from one another. A disturbed and imbalance parent rear unfit child for society and the cycle will perpetuate itself to indefinite as long as people are un-conscious and unaware.

Fear, The Central Weapon for Control

Striking fear into someone's heart rob them from internal strengths and resources make them vulnerable and weak. Human tends to adapt to the dreadful situation with employing an unconscious psychological mechanism called defense mechanism, that reduces anxiety from unacceptable or potentially harmful stimuli.

When we are facing atrocity and difficulties, the best way to cope with the dreadful situation is numbing out, which is the fundamental step for surviving. The only fear that human is not capable of tolerating, is fear of unknown. Human has the urge to know, having clarity about our lives empower us to face apprehension, but being confused and cloudy threatens our desire for stability and contentment. This is the common knowledge to organized religions, they surreptitiously pursue their agendas. Organized religions use ambiguity and illusion of past and future, heaven and hell to control mass. Religions do not promote mindfulness and living in the present moment in contrary masterfully have manufactured fictional stories and characters to twist the truth of our ancient spiritual teachings. Organized religions brain washes people and promote superstitious rituals.

Shame, fear, and guilt are commonly used tactics by religions to enslave humans. David Hawkins the widely known authority within the field of consciousness and spirituality, has outlined different levels of consciousness in relation with our emotions. In his book "power vs. Force, The Hidden Determinants of Human Behavior" (Hawkins, 2002), has noted that the lowest energy level of functioning is Shame and Guilt, in his scale of consciousness, the initial level of empowerment is at 200, Shame is 20 and Guilt is 30.

Fearful individuals unconsciously contribute in promoting cults and religions plans. They are faithful slaves with no awareness, they find existence of other beliefs threatening. Creating awareness around this notion, is essential to free humanity. .

War and Political Conflict

War is a reality in this world, and typically the underlying reason is either politic or religion. Warfare appears to become tribal, local, small-scale, widespread, vicious, and personal. World War I was the war in the battle line; the combatants were 95 percent of killed people. In recent years war involves civilian populations, and it has been estimated 90 percent of killed people due to ethnic, political, and religious wars and civilians.

War causes suffering for civilian, this suffering is called "collective stress" or "social suffering," which is, a stress condition that affects an entire group of people. Historically, psychology has focused on individual combatants in terms of addressing the psychological consequences of war and designing interventions to meet those needs. The psychological literature on the impact of war stress on civilians is scarce, and there is a lack of theoretical models, assessment tools, and psychologically based models for intervening at a large scale to aid civilian victims. After World War II, mental health professionals found urgency and desire to study real-world events. This has changed since Milgram (1964) was looking for an answer to know how humans could perpetrate such brutality and evil on other humans.

Jung, the father of psychoanalysis and psychiatrist, believed that the force of Rationalism had eroded man's spiritual values to a dangerous degree, leading to worldwide disorientation and dissociation. He said that we have become dominated by the goddess Reason, who is our most significant and most tragic illusion. He researched anthropological documentation regarding what happens when a society loses its spiritual values, he suggested that people miss the meaning of their lives, social organization disintegrates, and morals decay. Jung attributed this partially to religious leaders being more interested in protecting their institutions than understanding the mysteries of faith.

War has a significant effect and extreme traumatization on war survivors. The survivors as children and teenagers during the trauma exposure who survived the political violence will carry the trauma-related effects and memories to their adult lives without receiving any psychological interventions or help. These children will become adults who are making the society at large, and that leads to underlying anxiety, lack of connection and sense of community. These adults become parents who are raising children and cant provide emotional safety for their children to grow and thrive, they either become overprotective parents who halt kids' mental growth or they become so consumed with their own mental and thought processing which make ignorant parents.

Studies showed a group of children who were victims of witnessing political violence (holocaust), their memory of traumatic experience was retained in novelistic details. In these children, massive denial and repression was not evidence. I believe I was like them, I did remember all the horrific experiences and witnessing the most devastating events, but I could still manage to go through life and continue my social life and education and maintain a healthy relationship, I was able to keep my creativity and ambition.

I was not in denial, but I developed General Anxiety Disorder, I would go places and do things but always I was anxious, and I managed to live with anxiety. Ironically my anxiety banished as soon as I stepped out of Iran and immigrated to Sydney Australia. But what stayed with me was the alert state, the survivor archetype was alive and functioning all the time. I didn't realize that I was carrying a massive scar on my psyche since I didn't know what relief means. When I finally resolved my inner conflicts and internal struggles to maintain my illusion of safety by therapeutically working on my psyche, I realized that I was not living fully until then. The children who experienced holocaust or any children who suffer any other form of trauma become adults and might be able to manage to have normal lives but not free or healthy living.

In contrast in other studies, interview with adults who have been able to manage to stay alive during exposure to political violence was subsequently hospitalized and diagnosed as psychotic. Many of these patients became silent and did not speak to anyone. These victims did not remember their experiences. The memories of the horrific experiences were erased, or the memories have been registered and kept "frozen" in a different part of the brain that had no access to consciousness. The retrieval of the memory of feelings is essential for the survival of the self. The self is maintained through narrative affective memory, for the victims or witnesses who have lost their memories, regaining their psychological wellbeing is not possible.

We have two brain hemispheres, right and left brain. These two hemispheres have different functioning, and for an individual to have a balance and healthy life, the two regions need to work actively together at the same time and to communicate with one another. for example, the left brain processes the rational aspect of the situation while the right brain is processing the emotional response to the same situation. The left brain is responsible for analytical and problem solving and calculations and studying facts, and the right brain is responsible for emotions and creativity. Creative and emotional people have tendency to use their right hemisphere more, and the people with a rational mind to use their left brain more. Traumatic experiences are embedded in the right brain, and to have access to those memories, it is essential to activate those suppressed and repressed materials. There are techniques to enable both brain hemispheres while addressing life experiences such as EMDR, Eye Movement Desensitization and bilateral stimulation by use of art therapy techniques.

Exposure to Violence

When violence is ongoing, persistent and continuous, it may form an integral part of each individual's world, identity, values, beliefs, and history and not only affect a part of their present, but also inform who each person will become. As a result, it will invariably inform the community itself. When we look at the history of a specific group, we notice a pattern of behavior and the specific characteristic is shared among those people, which is ongoing and carries on for centuries. For example, if a society has identified with the victim role due to their past traumatic experiences, they are mostly consumed with the sense of safety and security, they lack trust and they primarily orient on fear and survival. Their culture and customs gradually form as their identity and as a group, they follow specific custom and traditions. This conditioning will create limitations and that society will have difficulty to thrive. They usually choose governments to continue the abuse and instill fear in them and often, they have a high tolerance for accepting the abusive laws and rules, and they get stuck with bad leaders and tyrants. To help these societies, it is crucial to help people to recover from that chosen or group trauma from the past and help them to identify the adverse effect and to resolve the internal struggles and move forward and liberate themselves from the intergenerational pain and suffering and brainwash.

PART 4
Huma Development

Human Life Stages and Development

The future safety of the world and the individual security of each one of us depends on children growing up into adults who are well-balanced, productive, committed to social development and nationhood-and who recognize diversity not as a threat to be eliminated, but as an enriching and shared human value. However, the challenge is that adolescence is a time of life faced with emotional instability and confusion, which generate problems for the adolescent, their family and society. Teenagers have a crucial role in forming the future of each society, since they are very close to adulthood and during these stage of identity formation, if they identify with humanistic characteristic and recognize their role as a human rather identifying with a social group or religion that control them with fear, and if they connect with their internal strengths and have a healthy sense of self and establish a secure schema about self, others and build a healthy self-esteem and self-confidence, therefor they will add to the value of that society. They will become better people for self and others, they develop constructive coping mechanism, the level of anxiety and depression in adulthood will decrease, they become proactive, more creative and productive, they will be able to form a healthy relationship with others, they become good parents and raise healthy children. In such society, people will be liberated, strong esteem and will have a strong sense of community.

There are nine essential tasks of development during adolescence as : emotional and psychological independence, self-definition or self-concept, self- motivation and self-determination, appropriate set of values to be used as self-control, the development of empathy and the practice of reciprocity, and sexual identity, development of new intellectual capacities and skills, relating to peers and age mates, engaging in a training program to develop skills for achieving economic independence. The establishment of a realistic self- concept (identity) is the most basic task of adolescence. Behavioral experimentation, the process through which much of the emotional growth of adolescence occurs, also accounts for the majority of the inconsistent and confusing actions that characterize the adolescent.

Piaget and Inhelder (1969) named the period in adolescence from age 11 and up as Formal Operation stage. At this stage the individual can think logically about abstract propositions and test hypotheses systematically. At this stage the adolescent becomes concerned with the hypothetical, the future, and ideological problems. As suggested by Erikson, the adolescence stage is marked from age 12-18 years. He has named this stage as Ego development outcome: Identity vs. Role confusion, basic strengths are Devotion and Fidelity. Up to 12 years the person's development mostly depends upon what is done to him/her. From 12 years and up the development primarily is upon what the person does, and while adolescence is a stage at which the person is neither a child nor an adult life gets more complex as the individual attempts to find out their own identity. One of the adolescents' tasks is struggle with social interactions, and struggle with moral issues. Erikson divided the stages of adulthood into the experiences of young adults, middle aged adults and older adults. Erikson's basic philosophy rest on two major themes: 1) the world gets bigger as we go along and 2) failure is cumulative.

The development is as a "spiraling cycle" rather than as stages. We come back to the stages that we have already passed in a spiral form. The idea of growth as a cycle is common to many cultures and religions including the Native American medicine wheel circle, ancient Egyptian and Persian doctrines, Taoism and Buddhism. These cultures have common perspectives which is a cycle based on nature—a rhythmic circle of seasonal growth and return.

The pattern of seven developmental stages is as follows; The first five stages cover the time period from birth to age 12. These stages are Being, Doing, Thinking, Identity and Skills. At about age 13 we enter stage 6, which is a recycling stage called Integration. This stage lasts until we are about 19 years old; it is a repeat of the first five stages but at twice the pace. The seventh stage covers all our adult years. Over the course of adulthood, we return to the themes and issues of the earlier stages with new opportunities to "grow through" the developmental issues each stage represents. We either encounter or can create opportunities to revisit each stage as many times as we need to.

Bandura the psychologist and scholar, who studied adolescent aggression, believed in "reciprocal determinism," that is, the world and a person's behavior cause each other. Bandura considered personality as an interaction between three components: the environment, behavior, and one's psychological processes. The interaction of the individual with the environment in social learning theory and the personality. Personality is not separable from the individual's environment. The personality is internal and also responsive to the external environmental stimuli. In order to understand a behavior, the consideration will be the individual (i.e., his or her life history of learning and experiences) and the environment (i.e., those stimuli that the person is aware of and responding to). Personality is a relatively stable set of potentials for responding to situations in a particular way.

The changes in an individual's behavior result from interaction effects between the environment and the individual. This includes how the environment affects the individual as well as how the individual affects the environment. Social circumstances also have an influence upon moral and ethical judgments and how these judgments influence behavior. Social learning theory states that an individual's social group is influential over the performance of unethical behaviors.

Whether it is intentional or not, social learning theory is being used to create future generations of terrorists. Based on this theory, behavior can be influenced by the reciprocal interaction between environmental, personal, and behavioral factors. This theory states that individuals can learn through the performance of their own actions, and by witnessing the actions of others. The core concepts of this theory include observational learning, reinforcement, behavioral capability, self-efficacy, and expectations. Behavioral capability and self-efficacy are achieved by recruiting young children and adolescents and training them in terrorist techniques. Expectations are an influence over behavior when people believe that community members will view their sacrifice in a positive manner. An individual who participates in a suicide bombing is being influenced by the environment and if this behavior is viewed positively by the community, the individual is influencing the environment through reciprocal determinism.

In conclusion brain washing children and adolescents by politicians and religions can turn them to killing machines with no possibility of transformation. It is up to us to increase our knowledge and awareness to protect our children.

PART 5
Trauma and it's Effects

Trauma

Traumatic events have different causes, but they are overwhelmingly horrifying, terrifying, and laden with death and/or the threat of death. When a person is severely traumatized, it is normal that they cannot take the extent of the experience they have undergone at once. The traumatized individual's view of the world is severely changed. Traumatized individual's mind is frequently unable to allow the full impact of the event into consciousness and the traumatic memory exists in a highly charged sensory state triggered in flashbacks, nightmares, and arousal states that occur with reminders of the original event.

According to the most revision of the Diagnostic and Statistical Manual of Mental Disorders (DSM V 20016), trauma has been characterized as when the person experienced, witnessed, or was confronted with an event or events that involve actual or threatened death, or serious injury, or a threat to the physical integrity or self or others. The person's response involves intense fear, helplessness, or horror. One of the aspects of trauma is the feeling of humiliation in regard with person's capacity to protect self or others. Traumatic experiences may include feelings of severe loss, anger, betrayal, and helplessness. Loss is always part of trauma; loss can be manifested in its symbolic form of loss of a sense of safety and security or in a form of specific loss, loved ones or property.

Loss creates emotional reactions, which are called "mourning" and "grief," grief creates responses of intrusive, distressing preoccupation with the deceased person in the form of yearning, longing, and searching, which in "traumatic grief" the intensity of these responses and the duration can dominate the bereaved person's life. The grief and mourning as a result of traumatic loss combines with fear and anxiety associated with the trauma, which interfere with normal bereavement. Horror of the traumatic event blocks the pre trauma memories.

All forms of trauma can cause survivors to conclude that the world is not and may never be the same because of what happened, but this conclusion can be particularly convincing after a deliberatively inflicted trauma. For some it leads to intense sense of distancing that, without treatment, can persist and negatively affect the individuals' future recovery. One form of loss is the loss of predictable future which is often the result of mass trauma.

Posttraumatic loss can involve mass destruction, bodily injury, death of love ones, and symbolic loss of sense of security about life and future and ability to trust other people. Each loss can generate expected psychological responses caused by threat on one's own life which leads to anxiety and depression. Loss trauma is the result of witnessing death or loss of loved one leading to grief and mourning. Responsibilities traumas is caused by failure to protect oneself or others which leads to the sense of guilt.

Mass Trauma

Mass trauma as when frightening, life threatening event is experienced by a group of people at the same time. People who are exposed to mass trauma will show different range of response to the traumatic event and it might include; confusion, rage, loss of belief in the goodness of humankind and other responses to acute stress and loss. War and civil/political/community violence and terrorism is one of the situations that can cause mass trauma.

Mass trauma event has two component, type I which is single traumatic event or acute, and type II which is recurring traumatic event or chronic or ongoing. Exposure to the traumatic event is considered either as on site, on the periphery, or through the media. Extend of exposure to the violence/injury/pain is as: witnessed or experienced, nature of losses/deaths/ or destruction and finally acknowledgment of causality which can be random act of God or deliberate/human-made. Both type of trauma I or II generates extreme fright and responses that, if untreated, can lead to serious disorders in both children and adulthood.

Reactions Following Trauma

Reactions directly following the traumatic event can be characterized as shock. Such reactions might include a feeling that nothing is real, emotional apathy and confusion, as well as physical responses such as trembling, shivering or nausea. Long-term consequences include fear, vulnerability, depression and pessimism, irritability and anger, sleep disorders, extreme fatigue or difficulty concentrating, as well as the repeated and uncontrollable reliving of the event itself.

Complex Trauma

The term complex trauma describes the dual problem of children's exposure to multiple traumatic events and the impact of this exposure on immediate and long-term outcomes. Complex trauma exposure results when a child is abused or neglected, but it can also be caused by other kinds of events such as witnessing domestic violence, ethnic cleansing, or war. Many children involved in the child welfare system have experienced complex trauma.

In middle childhood and adolescence, the most rapidly developing brain areas are those that are crucial for success in forming interpersonal relationships and solving problems. Traumatic stressors or deficits in self-regulatory abilities delay this development, and can lead to difficulties in emotional regulation, behavior, consciousness, cognition, and identity formation. Supportive and sustaining relationships with adults—or, for adolescents, with peers—can protect children and adolescents from many of the consequences of traumatic stress. When interpersonal support is available, and when stressors are predictable, escapable, or controllable, children and adolescents can become highly resilient in the face of stress.

Affect Regulation

Affect Regulation refers to the ability to interpret feelings rationally in defensive states.

Its intention is to produce an appropriate response in any given situation. Exposure to complex trauma can lead to severe problems with affect regulation, which begins with the proper identification of internal emotions. When a child is exposed to positive models of affect and behavior, they are better able to develop the ability to differentiate among states of arousal, interpret these states, and apply the appropriate labels. If children are exposed to conflicting examples of behavior or inconsistent responses to affect display no coherent framework is provided through which to interpret experience.

After identifying the emotional state experienced, children must then be able to accurately express their emotions and calm their internal mental state. Children exposed to complex and traumatic situations experience difficulty and impairment in both of these areas. Because of these difficulties children may display symptoms of dissociation, the chronic numbing of emotional experience. They may also develop dysphoria, maladaptive coping strategies, and begin avoiding of all emotional experiences, including positive experiences. Exposure to trauma during childhood increases the risk for major depression, and also appears to increase the duration of depression and shows a poorer response to standard treatments.

Dissociation

Dissociation is one of the key responses in victims of complex trauma and limits the capability of integrating emotions and experiences. It is a defense mechanism used to protect the mind by disconnecting thoughts and emotions. Physical sensations are outside conscious awareness and repetitive behavior occurs without awareness. Dissociation is one of the main coping mechanisms in the face of traumatic exposure and can develop into a problematic disorder, exacerbating difficulties with behavioral management, affect regulation, and self-concept.

There is a range of symptom as a result of exposure to complex trauma.

This exposure in early life associates with symptoms of Posttraumatic Stress Disorder and other symptoms which extend beyond PTSD. These symptoms and impairment are as follows:

(a) self-regulatory, attachment, anxiety, and affective disorders in infancy and childhood; (b) addictions, aggression, social helplessness and eating disorders; (c) dissociative, (d) somatoform, cardiovascular, metabolic, and immunological disorders; (e) sexual disorders, in adolescence and adulthood; and (e) re-victimization.

Post Traumatic Stress Disorder (PTSD)

PTSD affects many people following an event that involves death, serious injury, or threat to the physical integrity of the self or others. This person will experience feelings similar to extreme fear, helplessness and horror during and post the initial traumatic experience. The memories and emotions associated with the distressing event/events can continue affecting a person's life for years (DSM IV, 2000).

The following factors that affect/ increase the chances of developing PTSD in children:

- The trauma experienced is severe
- The parent's reaction to the trauma
- The distance separating the child from the trauma

Children and adolescents exposed to severe trauma tend to have the highest levels of PTSD. Symptoms decrease with the help of a positive support group. If a parent copes well with the trauma, the child will have more opportunities to heal by example. Children and adolescents who witness a traumatic event from a distance, might also experience lower levels of PTSD. While it is unclear how big of a part ethnicity plays in the development of PTSD, studies do show that minorities display higher levels of it, possibly because they are exposed to more trauma. Girls are also more likely than boys to develop PTSD.

Another factor consistently investigated in the ongoing research of PTSD in children is age. Some researchers believe the effects of trauma relative to age will appear different in the child exposed. PTSD symptoms in teens (ages 12-18) are sometimes difficult to classify as they are in between childhood and adulthood. Their behavior, while more closely resembling that of an adult, will be more impulsive and aggressive. That will indicate the level of undiagnosed PTSD in young adults that manifests itself as aggression, in driving, using and abusing drug and alcohol, risk taking behaviors, which will lead to the ultimate perception of self. They will identify themselves with as an angry and unhappy person, and usually they project their unhappiness on the social affairs, and they become the blamers in our society. They perceive everything as limitation toward their successes, they blame educational system, they become a solid believer that the society and government is corrupted and there is no job for them. They start hating immigrants or other hard-working social members, and this undiagnosed PTSD of them will control their lives forever like a dark shadow casting over their life and future.

Psychological, Physiological and Biological Effect of Trauma

Traumatizing experiences will activate a psychological defense mechanism, which helps the person to avoid the integration of the harmful stimuli with the consciousness at the time of exposure. The employed mechanism is known as dissociation. Exposure to trauma activates HPA axis that is an operation of neuro endocrine system in the body, this system helps the person to fly or fight the threatening situation, which helps the survivor during presence of prominent danger.

The concept of PTSD is a "physioneurasis" condition, which is a chronic body and brain multisystem functioning. The treatment of these chronic stages is challenging. PTSD condition involves multiple systems of the brain and body and can be progressive and self-perpetuating. Sometimes an environmental or stressful situation that can trigger PTSD symptoms will be mistakenly perceived as the original traumatic experiences. For example, when Eddie came to his first session and couldn't breath and he said he couldn't stop crying for four days after he found out that his close friend is attempting suicide. Eddie was successful to save his friend's ife but the traumatizing experience shocked his system to the point that he was trapped in freeze state. After a thorough assessment I realized that his case is not Acute Stress Disorder, but it is a PTSD symptoms which are triggered by the present experience. Undiagnosed PTSD leads to unsuccessful therapy. Trauma victims who are diagnosed with PTSD also suffer from some disease such as Irritable Bowel Syndrome, gastro-esophageal reflux disease, interstitial cystitis, chronic pain syndromes, fibromyalgia/CFS, and RSD. All of these diseases are compatible with a deregulated autonomic nervous system, especially with parasympathetic dominance. There are other diseases of stress, including hypertension, peptic ulcer disease, ulcerative colitis, and atherosclerotic coronary artery disease and the high cortisol-based diseases of stress . Prolong exposure to trauma and stress will affect the body which might cause initiation or to development and interrelate to many other chronic diseases with unknown causes.

Trauma as a 'Disease of Memory'

Psychologists suggest that human beings after exposure to trauma might lose the capacity to remember or lose their frame of reference. Memory is the way in which past experience is encoded in the brain and shapes present and future. After exposure to trauma, areas of the brain related to memory and emotional response may be damaged.

Trauma, Instinct, and the Brain: The Flight/Fight/Freeze Response:

Stress and trauma can complicate and interconnect responses of the brain, the hormonal system and behavior. Selye (1955) introduced the theory of a general adaptation syndrome (GSA) in response to prolonged stress. There are 3 phases in GSA; alarm, resistance, and exhaustion. During exposure to acute stress or trauma, the body displays acute flight/fight response.

Right brain is the pathway for the acute response to a threat. The parasympathetic nervous system is inactivated in extreme danger stimulation which plays a role in the freeze, or immobility response, fight/flight/ freeze sequence. The freeze response is a form of survival which helps animals to mimic death, releasing endorphins which has analgesic effects and has been known responsible cause of dissociation.

Freeze response cause Inescapable Shock (IS). It has been explored if animals are consistently exposed to life threatening situations, they will produce a consistent freeze in the face of manifest helplessness thus it leads to exhibition passive immobility. A freeze response triggered by a traumatic event may become linked to environmental cues through conditioning. Repetitive exposure to IS impairs basic storage of memory and information. The brain loses its ability to process the possible opportunities to escape in the case of IS.

Post-traumatic stress disorder may have a biological model in the reaction of animals to IS. A link between IS state in animals and dissociative state in human when facing sever life threats or trauma. In the freeze state, endorphin releases in high level which cause a freeze response and put an alert and responsive mind to sleep, the mind becomes dissociated. Memory access and storage are impaired, and amnesia might occur during the whole part or some of the relevant incidents to the events. Endorphin and parasympathic activities are responsible for the freeze and dissociation response, which follows with high activity of sympathic nervous system. In animals the freeze response is dangerous and life threatening and in humans will cause a sense of detachment numbness and even confusion in the face of traumatic event. Release of endorphins, during physical injury helps the brain to dull the pain sensation.

Many of post traumatic symptoms that surface after so many years from unresolved trauma experiences are the results of freeze response and dissociation. In the face of trauma, human may suppress their instinctual behavior which might imprint the traumatic experience in unconscious memory and arousal system of the brain. At the time of the traumatic event, the pattern of defensive and protective movement is stored in procedural memory to enforce adaptation for future related threats. This will lead the body to respond to a stimulus as the memory of pain and physical sensation years after the exposure.

Trauma in Children/Adolescents

Childhood trauma can be a factor in development of a number of disorders in childhood and adulthood. Childhood psychic trauma appears to be crucial etiological factor in the development of a number of serious disorders both in childhood and in adulthood. There are four characteristics related to childhood trauma that appear to last for long periods of life, 1) repetitive behaviors, 2) trauma-specific fears, 3) changed attitudes about people, life, and the future, 4) visualized or repeatedly perceived memories of the traumatic event.

Terr (1991) categorizes trauma in childhood to two types, type I trauma includes "full, detailed memories, "omens" and misperceptions. Type II trauma includes denial and numbing, self hypnosis and dissociation, and rage . Trauma begins with the events outside the child. Once the events take place, a number of internal changes occur in the child which last. The changes stay active for years-often to the detriment of the young victim. According to Herman and Van Der Kolk, the behavioral reenactment may recur so frequently as to become distinct personality traits. These may eventually gather into the personality disorders of adulthood, or they may recur so physiologically as to represent what seems to be physical disease. Traumatized children feel that their vulnerability and their "shield of invincibility" becomes broken, and they feel threatened by the future and perceive it as an upcoming threat.

Consequences of Unresolved Trauma Experiences Bio/Psycho/Social

The most common complaint in current medical practice, that of persistent and unexplainable chronic pain, has its roots in the persistent changes in brain circuitry associated with unresolved trauma, and the continued tendency for dissociation to occur in the face of stress or threat. In a case study that the effects of anxiety and fear inhibit the process of differentiation and the integration and balancing of cognition and affect. He illuminates the differentiation process of a woman at midlife who is struggling with her needs of self-versus others due to her unresolved trauma experiences. A study of long-term impact 20 years after high school students as hostage by Desivilya, Gal, & Ayalon, in year 1996, revealed that although most survivors exhibited relatively high levels of adaptation, the traumatic experience at adolescence had a long-lasting effect on the survivor's adult life. This effect has been noted in intrapersonal and interpersonal domains, as well as in their emotional response in emergency situations, such as the Gulf War.

Volcan (2004) used three terms to define the potential for unresolved trauma on groups of people. Injuries deliberately inflicted upon a large group of people by an enemy group have been labeled as "Massive large group trauma". Volkan found that groups of people subjected to this variety of trauma suffer extreme losses and often experience emotions related to shame, humiliation, and helplessness. They also struggle with an inability to assert themselves. The unresolved trauma is the reason that these victims cannot successfully mourn these extreme losses or cope with their feelings. Residue from the trauma can be seen in behavior when they tend not to assert themselves effectively in politically or socially adaptive ways. One of the most devastating issues with unresolved trauma is that they almost always end up internalizing a sense of helpless rage and idealizing masochism. These victims are prone to maladaptive sadistic outbursts and the community at large generally shares these manifestations.

Future generations are expected to resolve the psychological tasks that their parents did not, and struggle with these transmissions. As these intergenerational transmissions take place, the shared memory of the historical trauma may evolve into "chosen trauma" . Chosen traumas become significant markers for the large- group identity. As time and future generations evolve, "Chosen traumas" sometimes create a foundation for the society's development of an exaggerated entitlement ideology that, under attack or threat to a group's identity, can be manipulated by political leaders to develop new political programs or social paradigms that support this ideology. This belief system deemed by Volkan as "exaggerated entitlement", asserts that the group has a right to own what they wish to have.

Memories of the Holocaust affect the present and most sensitive phases of the life cycle of future generations, this includes: reproduction, productivity, and creativity. All families affected by the Holocaust experience residual trauma, including the men and women who were indirectly involved, such as in witnessing the atrocities. Survivors of the Holocaust have displayed self-image as well as a displayed fragmented self in the arts that they made, this self fragmentation was the result of the massive trauma they witnessed. The fragmented self in survivors became evident while they were interviewed about their experiences; most of them used "I" without noticing they were actually speaking about themselves. Trauma can influence future family relations and create challenges in intimacy.

PART 6
Witnessing Political and Religious Violence

Political Violence

Political violence is a "phenomenon that has particularly devastating and destructive consequences at many different levels and realms. It refers to a wide range of acts and events perpetrated either by the state (in case of authoritarian, corrupt and repressive regimes) or by anti-state, subversive factions or individuals.

Any form of political violence with any origin creates a sense of invasive anxiety, disturbance, confusion and helplessness. Individuals face difficulties of predict and efficiently protecting themselves from sense of danger. The experience leaves them vulnerable and powerless and generates a sense of insecurity, unsafety, and instability which negatively affects the entire society. Living in communities exposed to political violence negatively affect people's interpersonal relationships and also their own individual intrapsychic worlds.

Under the political violence climate, people relate to each other's differently. They might relate to each other by act of suspicion, prejudice, which results in hostility among individuals of opposite political persuasions. At the same time, people who hold the same political views could bond deeper than ordinary friendships. Politic clearly is a calculated plan to pursue certain goal which benefits a certain group who are in power, the follower of a specific political party are usually the group who have needs and wants and are hoping their group or team will grant their wish as long as they destroy the opposing party. In this manner more division happens among people in a society and that gives people good enough excuses not to reach out to help other human being, nonetheless, hurting each other. The division in a society makes people in those society vulnerable and even more confused and keeps them distracted from the main issue that their people in power or their government is serving only a specific group at the cost of society. This division and confusion create slavery, people would not know who to hold responsible when their government is making mistake. They need always an opposing presented to them which can cut their profit, they introduce a label and a new name for those group, as soon as those civilians are named differently than the known political party, people perceive them as they not us, then whatever comes or proposed from them is rejected without any consideration, since it is them not us.

Any characterization of a violent event as political can be problematic and complex. Such characterization depends on a wide variety of factors, variables, and perspectives. These include the sociopolitical position of the observer, the intended function of the characterization, its location in a series of other related actions and events, etc., all of these are situated within the wider sociopolitical realities at the given time and place. When we are witnessing a violent act, even if we do not experience it directly in real life but we hear or read about it or view it on television, our response will have 4 characteristics, all of which are closely interlinked; it is likely to be emotionally charged, polarized, simplistic, and unpredictable.

Emotionally Charged Response

Violence events have a powerful emotional impact on individuals, engaging them personally. Individuals who are exposed to violence become biologically and psychologically alert. It is impossible for one not to respond instinctively to political violence. Actual distance in terms of time and space and the degree of the person's involvement with the violence, don't prevent the individuals from responding emotionally. Political violence creates a powerful vortex which tends to pull the observer in, and the reason is the process of identification.

Emotional response creates a feeling of instability and that often stimulates a hostile reaction, which may lead to turmoil and disorder. Individuals are likely to react (mostly unconsciously) to counteract this dis-order with an imposed order that attempts to limit the feared damage. For that reason they have no choice to try to stay calm and rational. As the result of these compulsive emotional reactions, individuals will have difficulty for openness, reflection and flexibility.

People who are exposed to political violence act impulsively and that limit their creative response and they become rigid and compulsive in their thoughts and actions. This emotionally charged responds result in more chaos and emotional irrationality thus escalating destructiveness. Therefore the destructiveness that political violence creates is not only produced by the violent acts themselves but also by the responses they create in bystanders and observers.

Traumatic loss is common during war. A study on the effect of war trauma on Chechnya, notes that in normal time and nurturing upbringing, most individuals hold "world assumptions." The assumptions include; benevolence, meaningfulness of the world, and a sense of self-worth. The exposure to horrifying and terrifying human injury and cruelty challenges these assumptions and they are completely shattered and hard to rebuild (Janof-Bulman 1992).

Witnessing and Polarized Response

A person involved with or witnessing political violence has a tendency to make judgment and evaluate the division between 'good' and 'bad,' 'safe' and 'unsafe,' and 'us' or 'them'. Kalmanowitz and Lloyd suggest that violence leave us to see things as 'black' or 'white.' We have a tendency to impulsively respond to self-preservation and choose the safest option in the quickest possible time. The polarized response happens when we are exposed to violence by direct exposure or through media, reading, or hearing about it. Our reactions to witnessing the violence, creates our identification with the victim's fear and suffering, which leads to intense psychological pressure in us. This identification creates a need for us to instantly end the pain and suffering. Political violence creates emotional reactions in the viewer that is difficult to separate his/her pain from that of the actual victims of violence. The viewer then either would identify with the victim or would identify with the aggressor in order to end the psychological pressure that is experiencing due to the act of violence and crime. The viewer might even experience a dark fascination. The identification with the aggressor is a form of defense mechanism to replace the sense of helplessness with the sense of control and power. Identifying with the victim might block the overwhelming pain in us, and identifying with the aggressor and being fascinated with the violence creates another set of psychological reactions.

This polarization can cause a strong sense of hate and leads the person to an extreme sense of polarization and violence. No matter how a person tries to use rationalization or justification, a strong sense of "us" and "them" is present.

Witnessing political violence creates a polarized response in the observer that makes the person lose the capability to act based on his/her fullest psychological, human, intellectual and political abilities. Simplification promotes stagnation and consequently further destruction.

People exposed to political violence act impulsively, which can shock them, it can cause irresponsible actions and feelings, it can detach them from their values, positions and even themselves. The unpredictability of their responses can result in "hot" type of reactions that keeps them closer to numbness, dissociation, un-relatedness, and even apathy. The longer the political violence lasts, the more alienation and dehumanization increase in social levels.

Religious Violence

> "It is chilling to see how belief in a future heaven creates a present hell."
>
> *Ekhart Tolle*

Jung (1971) believed that the worldwide challenge of disorientation and dissociation was partially instigated by the force of Rationalism, which he felt eroded man's spiritual values to a dangerous degree. People are dominated by the goddess Reason, who is the most tragic illusion. Some societies have historically dismissed its original spiritual values and have become rancid in moral, loss of confidence in regard to the purpose of life, and degradation in social organization. Jung attributed this, in part to spiritual leaders that had greater interest in protecting their institutions than in the mysteries of faith.

Religious extremism is a critical component of contemporary terrorism and political violence. Religiously motivated terrorists unlike politically motivated terrorists are more likely to conduct mass casualty attack. Religious extremists are not inhibited by the fear that excessive violence will offend some population, they serve their own ideology which put them in a position of us against them, and they view people as godly and sinful, who must be destroyed. Religiously motivated terrorists might even be willing to use weapons of mass destruction in their attacks.

In a study in Algeria, children and adolescents are often and unfortunately targets of terrorism if they develop in a war faring climate. These children witness collective massacres and few of them escape unmarked. In Islamic countries, schoolgirls are sometimes killed for not wearing the required chador or headscarf; their teachers have been executed for refusing to accept the 'diskats' of the terrorists. Women living in Algeria are often victims of Fatwa. Terrorist Muslim extremists declare Fatwa, which permits and incites the murder of babies, children and adolescents to prevent a future society they see as immoral.

School massacres have become commonplace and terrorists have even been known to throw babies into ovens. Females, little girls as well as women who live in Aljeri, suffer the worst form of terrorism: rape. Rape is also authorized by the 'Fatwa', which defines it as a 'pure act,' a marriage of pleasure. Collective rapes conceive the most terrible form of suffering. It is not uncommon for a woman's throat to be slit after rape. However, if she does survive and become pregnant, she will be ostracized by society. In addition to the moral and physical abuse inflicted upon these women by the traumatic consequences of rape, they are further inhibited by their family's rejection, which is common. This leads them to fall prey to depression, drug abuse, prostitution and suicide (Donelly et al., 2004).

Psychological Effects of Political and Religious Violence

The degree of psychological damage of individuals is proportional to the intensity, severity and duration of the exposure to the traumatic experiences. The degree of unpredictability, devastation and brutality of the violent event can produce more intense psychological damage.

Individuals are psychologically different; each individual has their unique personal history, family, community, culture and sociopolitical context, as well as with their distinctive psychological make-up and combination of their own strengths and weaknesses. As the result there are different reactions of exposure to political violence; psychological injuries that can lead to an actual pathological condition of shorter or longer duration and or resilience response.

There are people who could transform their experience in a positive way, finding new strengths and experiencing transformative renewal. Some resilient individuals who survived witnessing horrific violence experiences may respond to adversity in different ways in different contexts in their lives. These people have the mental capacity to separate themselves from the traumatic memories and move forward in their lives which I was one of them, but at some point, if they don't address the trauma that they have encountered, they won't be able to reach their fullest life potentials.

Brutal practices in armed forces suspension of human rights, poor living and working condition, including deprivation of food and warmth, beatings, humiliations, torture, abuse- cause mental health damage to the people who are involved with that political or religious organization. Those more profoundly affected are the young recruit, often straight from school. In Military, these young soldiers suffer inhuman treatment for 2 years and then are released back into society with no vocational training, their sense of right and wrong destroyed, and often suffering from Post-Traumatic Stress Disorder. These young soldiers in their desperation and traumatized state turn to criminality, drug abuse, and even suicide.

The grief processes

In the case of major trauma, the mourning process becomes impossible. Liftton writes of this when referring to the effects of the atom bomb dropped on Hiroshima. In cases of mass destruction, the incomprehension is such that there is no pain instead, it is replaced with a numb sensation-an anesthesia. It is impossible to mourn for six million, especially when there are no graves. It is also impossible to cope with the guilt of surviving.

During times of trauma, experiences may not be processed in symbolic or linguistic forms but may be organized and remembered as sensorimotor or images. Van der Kolk lists the symptoms as horrific images, visceral sensations, or fight/flight reactions. These can be reactivated by affective, auditory or visual cues leaving people in a state of extreme fear, therefore making it particularly difficult to access these events. The experience does not fit into existing conceptual schemata, cannot be accommodated or assimilated; it therefore overwhelms.

War may result in mass violent death. Also, military family members, who do not position to war zones, may still be exposed to attacks or disaster- subsequently to death and the injury. Military leaders have long recognized the potential for social isolation and so has developed a rich network of military community programs, support groups, and morale, welfare, and recreation. The military families in military community become "extended family" defined more by mutual understanding and shared values than by bloodline or marital relater operations. Any death and trauma can affect the extended community.

They may confront impending or immediate threat to life, the sudden and unanticipated loss of friends and loved ones. Military members and their families are also at risk for the emotional disturbances of exposure to violent death in the aftermath of an attack. The aftermath of traumatic loss (e.g., depression, acute stress disorder, posttraumatic stress disorder, and complicated grief) may be the result of exposure to war and attack for the military members and their families. A study on military communities reported that after math or attack and violent death there was a strong relationship between traumatic exposure and medically unexplained physical symptoms.

Post war syndromes as increase somatic complaints and disability in survivors of the Murrah building bombing. After any act of political violence, citizens experience mental and physical symptoms. People lose their confidence in the government's ability to protect its citizens and serve the goal of terrorism.

Mental and physical complaints in the aftermath of mass violent death

Symptoms related to the aftermath of mass violence are as follow: Acute stress disorder, Post traumatic stress disorder, generalized anxiety disorder, Panic disorder, Major depressive disorder, Brief psychotic episodes, Adjustment disorders, Complicated grief, Normal bereavement, Alcohol abuse, Substance abuse. Distress such as, Anger and irritability, Fear, Restlessness, Concentration and attention difficulties, Intrusive thoughts or images, Sadness, Insomnia (with or without nightmares). Somatic complaints include headaches, gastrointestinal distress, musculoskeletal pain. In extension with the above symptoms, there also are distress related behaviors such as increased alcohol or tobacco use, avoidance of work place/responsibilities, avoidance of travel, and social withdrawal.

Political Violence and the Psychological Effect on Children and Adolescents

Traumatic experiences occur during the war and post-war period, and children and adolescents are exposed to be different kinds of stress. They are usually long-lasting and have, as a consequence, a cumulative negative effect on the physical and mental development, emotions and intelligence as well as the morale of the child. The war related traumatic experiences causes children to be intimidated or horrified, killed, injured, tortured, imprisoned, physically and emotionally abused, forcefully recruited to participate in violent acts against fellow villagers and even their own families, malnourished, disabled, physically separated from their families, displaced, and orphaned by present-day armed conflicts. Uncertainties about the types of damage and the duration of the war add to the impact on children as well as their caregivers. Children also suffer the most when basic social needs (i.e, economy, public health, medicine, education, and social services) collapse.

Drastic changes in daily routines during wartime result in children's being confined indoors for most (if not all) of the day, limiting play and other recreational activities and promoting feelings of isolation and boredom. Their sleep may be interrupted by sirens and moving to shelters of sealed rooms. Some must take over the responsibility of an absent parent. The prolonged closure of schools deprives children of educational opportunities as well as additional school-related activities and routines that signify life stability (e.g., important regular social ties, social support of their peers, the reassurance of their teachers, and the steadying influence of familiar structures and routines). Schools often reopen before the dangers have entirely passed; as a result, lessons may be interrupted by various emergencies. Pupils must deal with fears, anxiety, fatigue, lack of concentration and, for some, a parent's absence.

Home is a symbol of familiarity, intimacy, and inviolability of the self; thus, the loss of a home has a deep personal meaning for children. Losing their home also involves losing significant social ties and support. Children may arrive at evacuation centers or refuges campsites in a state of shock. They may experience a high health risks due to crowded and unsanitary conditions. They also may refuge to other countries and face new cultures and challenges. By studying Kuwaiti children following the Gulf War, there are report that there is a link between proximity to war violence and increased self-reported somatic symptoms and complaints. Diastolic blood pressure was associated with the level of exposure to trauma and an inverse relationship was found between the presence of re-experiencing symptoms and somatic complaints and diminished interest in activities.

A global negative effect of war trauma on adolescent's development is the lower self-concept and higher levels of anxiety, clinical depression, isolation, somatic complaints, social problems, problem thinking, and delinquent behavior. Also The cognitive development damages as a result of exposure to war and PTSD, affecting both verbal and non verbal skills in children and adolescence. Children who are exposed to continued traumatic stress might suffer from the chronic and long-term nature of developmental damage. Refugee adolescents are developing strategies in the context of diverse, political, cultural, economic, and social forces that interact with the developmental needs of identity, self-image, increased autonomy, relations with peers, school achievement, and career goals.

For adolescents the war trauma becomes more complicated which puberty can have been delayed or experienced as "left out." Some of the people with war experiences during adolescents would claim that they have lost their teenage years. Individuals who experience war during their adolescence would either show some qualities that belong to the so-called latency period, or return to these values after an invisible attempt to attain a more mature developmental level.

Children and adolescents have been largely the forgotten victims of war. In fact, researchers had neglected the study of the psychological impact of war stress on children and adolescents until the 1990's, younger the victim, the greater the risk of psychological impairment. Adolescents with war experiences in the past and living with adults who have experienced the war and never seek psychological help at the time of the exposure, their traumatic experiences will never be put into words and stays unresolved.

Children who witness extreme acts of violence are at significant risk of developing anxiety, depressive, phobic, conduct, and post traumatic stress disorders. If a child suffers personal injury during act of violence in war will also develop numerous post traumatic symptoms, in addition to loosing trust in adults as protectors and developing negative, demoralized ideas about people, life, and the future. War-related experiences expose children to high levels of stressors during a critical time in their psychosocial development. War event may hinder on psychosocial development, notably hold backing interpersonal trust, elevating anxiety levels, and limiting the threshold for stress endurance.

Immediately following war, individuals reveal high level of stress reactions including fears, anxiety, hyper sensitivity, moderate levels of depression. High levels of exposure lead to greater subjective distress for children. Commonly reported stress reactions include fears, anxiety, hypersensitivity, moderate levels of depression, and increased dependency on parents. Predominant emotion reactions tend to be rage, hatred, and despair.

Physical injuries to children may cause loss of control, loss of self image, dependency, sigma, isolation, abandonment, and anger. Even minor wounds can create considerable risk for PTSD in children. The injured part of the body may act as a constant reminder of the trauma and interfere with the processing and resolution of traumatic experience. Some children have a tendency to dwell on the death and injuries of other family members and fellow victims, rather than on their own injuries. Adolescents may be particularly traumatized by their wounds because for them, the smallest imperfection is of enormous significance.

Late adolescence is a time when sociopolitical influences on identity are particularly powerful. A political ideology and commitment may help buffer the experience of war. Adolescents may interpret their experience as "necessary evil" that must be endured if ideological objectives are to be achieved.

Several studies have found that children with high exposure to a war reported significantly more adverse emotional, cognitive, and physiological symptoms than those residing in areas less exposed to war events and may sustain more long term damage. In contrast, some children remain highly anxious; changing their physical distance to the war does not necessarily change the psychological distance to it.

Childhood trauma can be a factor in developmental of a number of disorders in childhood and adulthood. Childhood trauma can lead to a definable mental condition. There are 4 characteristics related to untreated childhood trauma that can last long life. They consists of repeated visualization or other returning perceptions, repeated behaviors and bodily responses, trauma-specific fears, and revised ideas about people, life, and the future.

Trauma in childhood is categorized to two major types: type I which is brought on by one sudden shock, including full, detailed memories, "omens", and misperception and type II, which is precipitated by a series of external blows, which includes denial and numbing, self-hypnosis and dissociation, and rage. Exposure to war trauma can lead to ego developmental issues and physical manifestation of the chronic trauma.

PTSD as the Result of War in Children

Some individuals who are exposed to war, political violence or acts of terrorism do develop mental health problems as a result of their experiences and are often labeled with the psychiatric term Post Traumatic Stress

Disorder. Predictors of PTSD in wartime include levels of personal (first hand) exposure to war, proximity to traumatized people, subjective impact of the trauma, and negative social support structures after war. Violence-related disasters have been consistently linked to PTSD and related symptoms in children, adolescents, and adults. Acts of violence may lead to PTSD in children and youth as well as to co-morbid problems with anxiety and depression.

Children exhibit a wide-ranging accommodation to war situations and some of children go on to develop chronic PTSD after war. Growing up in a war-affected community appears to promote aggressive behavior in some children, one potential consequence of the long duration of some wars is that children may minimize or habituate to war-related distress.

If violence is perpetrated by someone who looks "average," such as a neighbor or classmate, children may not know whom to trust or how to evaluate who is dangerous. If violence is perpetrated by an unknown assailant, the experience may challenge children's beliefs that adults can and will protect them, in either situations the child's sense of trust in damaged.

PART 7
Resiliency

Coping Strategies

There is numerous family and society related factors and psych-socio-physiological processes that protect child development and mental health. These protective factors as; Loving and wisely guiding parenting, children's flexible and high cognitive capacity, Flexible and multiple coping strategies, Narrative and symbolic nocturnal dreaming, social support, and good peer relations.

For children who are exposed to war related trauma coping is mainly affect regulation, whereas in other disasters coping tends more toward revision of situation. The impact of war stress on children depends on both personal coping capacity and environmental support. Young children's resilience depends considerably on their parents' stress absorption and their parents' and significant others' support. Since during war time the main impact of war stress and disaster is on parent's shoulder in order to survive and protect their lives and children's lives, parents display tremendous amount of emotional reactivity and fear, and kids have no choice to experience the trauma of war first hand dealing with their own fears and second hand dealing with their parents fear and lack of adequate support. In children brain is not developed fully and children up to certain age have no abstract thinking, if the appropriate emotional and psychological support is not present during the exposure to war trauma or any traumatic experiences, these children get the most damaging experience.

For older children and adolescents, individual dispositions and interpretations of their situational (and environmental) control play a greater part. For adolescents, war often brings out a strength and energy unlike anything seen at other times. Coping behavior can be directed at managing the stressor itself (i.e. active or problem-focused coping), avoiding the stressor (i.e. avoidance coping), and reducing the aversive emotional reactions resulting from exposure to stress (i.e. emotion-focused or palliative coping.

During war, problem-focused coping is concentrated in actions to improve safety. Behaviors designed to reduce the emotional impact of the situation (i.e. avoidance and emotion-focused coping) become vital in low control situations to help reduce or relieve anxiety. Children minimize the distress induced by disaster situations and wars through distancing, distraction, disengagement, wishful thinking, or denial to attempt to reduce the scary feelings of war.

The defensiveness may offer temporary protection when the situation cannot be controlled, allowing the children the needed time to assimilate the experience. It is possible that the habituation may be a coping mechanism that is more available to those not directly hit or who experience war from a relative safe distance. Children with a cause were better able to focus some of their energy in a positive capacity (e.g. caring for the disabled), rather than feel lonely, isolated, or without purpose. A cause creates a central life theme and thus enhances a sense of commonality, creates a commitment to cooperate and take some action when possible, thus enhancing a sense of control over one's destiny, and enables a focus on a better future.

Children most probably could not grasp the magnitude of what they were going through during war. All the adults interviewed by Kaplan had some memories that they could not let go of, which lead to a strong uneasiness or anxiety. For older children, ideology may contribute to coping in war like situations. Adolescents are able to make use of ideology as a personal resource and of resilience. Conversely, when ideological commitment turns rigid (e.g. through propaganda), it may exacerbate and sustain justification of violent acts by children; in some places older children become active protagonists of war as a result. Thus, it is important to consider the extent to which children should be exposed to ideological propaganda. It was also suggested that religion and prayer may have an instrumental meaning attached to them.

A sense of humor promotes coping with emotional strain and

providing mental lagging against being overwhelmed. In war, humor allows immediate and spontaneous catharsis without directly revealing specific personal fears: Humor promotes a partial denial of fears; and a sense of mastery through reframing, making some sense of a chaotic experience, letting out aggression towards the enemy, and strengthening group togetherness and morale. Children gain a sense of control over their lives by being involve in helpful behaviors. By helping others, their minds keep off the dangers and the war. Children should be trained with age relevant activities they can help with at home, in school, and in the community. Children were encouraged to get involved in art work and art exhibition. The activities enabled them to ventilate feelings and kept them occupied, active, and creative as well.

Children must gain positive expectations. The lack of (or the limited) experience with the adversities of war and the war being a prolonged crisis, may lead children to exaggerate their problems and prevent them from seeing a better future. Most children cope successfully and manage to adapt despite the circumstances they encounter. There are some positive role of war stress, such as the times when people experience cohesiveness with their family and peers more than they did before or when they initiate successful and, sometimes, courageous behaviors that increase their self-esteem.

In a number of refugee settings, and work with survivors of political violence, the crucial role of community, family and or social networks in individuals' recovery from massacre and torture as well as in their ability to cope with their here-and-now experiences. People recover most effectively when their experiences are validated and when social cues strengthen their sense of healing. Like other violent disasters, war presents many risk factors for PTSD and other mental health effects. Those children exhibit wide-ranging accommodations to war situations and reports that only a minority of children goes on to develop chronic PTSD after war, However, that growing up in a war-affected community appears to promote aggressive behavior in some children, one potential consequence of the long duration of some wars (e.g., the conflict in Israel and Northern Ireland) is that children may minimize or habituate to war-related distress.

The experience of terror or horror in the face of a traumatic event represents a state of helplessness, which also maintains the essential state of impending freeze. Brain releases chemical and physical response to trauma which causes a state of perceived helplessness or freeze. Children require a certain level of cognitive development to comprehend deaths and violence. Making sense of war event is possible only within a religious and spiritual framework. The survivors are reported to re-evaluate the meaning of life in existential and spiritual terms. Survival involves a deeper grasp of the significance of life.

Gender Differences

Studies have shown that girls have greater distress levels than boys. Girls reported receiving higher level of social support than boys; girls who receiving low levels of social support had the highest levels of psychological distress. Thus, although girls may be at greater risk of distress, that risk may be minimized by enhancing levels of social support and permitting them to express their feelings and fears to others while they confront and deal with reminders of war experience, in most societies boys' emotional responses to traumatizing experiences is suppressed. Different cultures have assigned taugher roles to boys and they are perceiving themselves as heroes or soldiers or men of war. Thus facing traumatizing experiences in boys will cause more severe mental and psychological damage since they have no outlet to express freely their fears and anxiety, if so they will be judged by their culture and society as a weak person.

Parental Behavior and Response to Trauma and Effects on Children

The family plays a crucial role in determining how the child adapts to experiencing trauma. Factors which influence the child's level of traumatization is related to family environment, parental response to the traumatic event or disclosure, parent's history of their own childhood trauma and or parental psychopathology. In the aftermath of trauma, parental support is a key mediating factor in determining how children adapt to victimization. Familial support and parental emotional functioning are strong factors that work against the development of PTSD symptoms, as well as enhance a child's capacity to resolve the symptoms.

The response of the child's social support system, and predominantly the child's mother, is the most important factor in determining outcome of the child's reaction to the trauma. There are three main issues in parents' responses to their children's trauma: Believing and validating their child's experience, 2) tolerating the child's affect, and 3) Managing their own emotional response (www.NCTSNet.org).

Young children are influenced most heavily by the attitudes and actual responses of their caregivers; therefore, it is important for children not to be separated from their natural support system. In order to help children to adapt to the war circumstances, the intervention should aim at providing caregivers with the resourcefulness to help children. For older children and adolescents, both parents and educators play a vital role in buffering the experience of war and determining children's responses to the adversities of war. Adolescents are less dependent than young children on their parents and tend to respond more to the world beyond their families.

Emotional response displayed by the adults in the child's life (and not the war situation itself) was the best predictor of children's response after World War II. Children were more distressed by separation from their parents than by exposure to bombings or witnessing destruction, injury, or death. Even those who experienced constant bombing did not seem adversely affected, provided that they remained with their mothers or mother substitutes and the familiar routines continued.

Children exposed to war trauma are protected through family cohesiveness and positive home environment. There is an association between parent's and children's general psychopathology following war and political conflict, and this relationship can vary at different stages in the child development. Exposure to war trauma impacts on both parents' and children's mental health and their emotional responses are interrelated. Children can be affected directly by exposure to trauma and by adult's reactions, which is through primary and secondary traumatization. Some mechanism of direct impact have been found to apply independently to both parents and children such as loss of control, loss of self-image, fears of death and harm, and isolation from their social networks. Children can also experience increased dependency and fear of abandonment.

Media and Secondary Traumatization

The most common traumatic events reported by Palestinian children were, seeing victim pictures on television, and witnessing. The media coverage of the bombing event, its aftermath, and the subsequent criminal trials was unrelenting, especially in Oklahoma City, and PTSD symptoms were found to be higher among youth who spent much of their television time watching bombing-related programming. People who are living on the periphery or far away from the place of war or mass trauma is taking place they still become affected through the detailed and repeated media coverage that literally brought the traumatic events into the living rooms of the viewer. This could qualify as "vicarious traumatization" since is consisted of the secondary exposure to traumatic events through verbal and visual representation of scenes of horror. The power of the media is uncontrollable and potentially dangerous. It influence individual's perception of current events and forms their attitude towards other people particularly those from different backgrounds or cultures. Media coverage on different political party and news, when are presenting war scenes, are designed to brain wash people and to manipulate mass toward their specific agenda. Media is never neutral and in their coverage of war they need to follow specific order, the presentation.

Multi-Cultural Issues of Children in Response to Trauma

Assessment of trauma history and PTSD outcomes should always occur in a cultural context that includes the background, community, and modes of communication that both the assessor as well as the family brings to their interaction. Exposure to different types of trauma is variable across diverse ethno-cultural backgrounds (i.e., exposure to war/genocide, family violence, community violence, child maltreatment). In addition, people of different cultural, national, linguistic, spiritual, and ethnic backgrounds define key trauma-related constructs in many different ways and with different expressions (e.g., flashbacks may be "visions," hyperarousal may be "attacque de nerves," dissociation may be spirit possession). The threshold for defining a PTSD reaction as "distressing" or as a problem warranting intervention differs not only across national and cultural groups, but also within subgroups (e.g., geographic regions of a country with different sub-cultures; different religious communities within the same geographic area). As a result, psychometric assessment with standardized measures may confront children and families with questions that are considered unacceptable, irrelevant, incomplete, or simply incomprehensible.

Complex Trauma, Ethnicity and Culture

Cultural factors may influence children's developmental differences in ability to comprehend and communicate social concepts, the distinction between self and others, and the ability to symbolize and to access working or long term memory. In some cultures children are socialized to view intentionality and causality as attributes of collective groups rather than of individuals in isolation. If such children are sexually molested, they may not disclose the abuse because it might threaten their acceptance as a valued member of their families and communities. This acceptance may be perceived as more crucial to recovery than having the ability to say "no" or knowing how to counteract self-blaming thoughts or self soothe if feeling overwhelmed.

Interventions for prevention or treatment of children or adolescents' posttraumatic impairment typically have been developed within the context of the Western medical model. However, evidence based models such as cognitive-behavior therapy, Eye Movement Desensitization and Reprocessing (EMDR), or parent-child dyadic psychotherapy are eminently adaptable to address not only developmental, but also ethno-cultural, differences. For instance, it is possible to incorporate features designed to strengthen culture-specific resilience factors derived from empirical studies of children in different cultures who have been exposed to different types of complex trauma (e.g., mental flexibility among Palestinian children, coping resources of South African children, social support among African American children).

Naturalistic healing resources are also potentially vital to children's recovery from complex trauma. There are many native cultural mechanisms for addressing the disruptions of affect regulation, sense of meaning or connection that result from complex trauma. Finally, prevention and treatment interventions also must consider the impact of racism and political/ethnic/class oppression as traumatic stressors.

Few empirical and psychological efforts have focused specifically on the topic of multicultural issues in disaster-exposed children youth. The Caucasian samples have received considerably greater research attention than have culturally and ethnically diverse populations. SES, social support, and culturally relevant beliefs and customs are just three of a large number of risk and protective factors that have been linked to psychological outcomes, such a temperament, genetics, gender, birth order, intelligence, and age, also religiosity/spirituality.

SES, and an inadequate level of social support can function as a risk factor for developing psychopathology in children after exposure to traumatic events. Social support can serve as a means for restoring lost resources, thus promoting better psychological adjustment after the occurrence of a traumatic event. Following the war in Bosnia and Croatia, many adolescent refugees refused to return home, in direct conflict with their parent's wishes.

This refusal could be explained by the greater educational opportunities in their host country together with the developmental need for independence; it also could be that their homes had become reminders of their traumatic war experiences. Transference does not just refer to unresolved infantile conflicts, confusions or deficits from childhood which are certainly key to the psychotherapeutic relationship, but also cultural and historical conflicts, confusions and deficits which may have affected generations before. These might include for example political oppression, social and economic inequality, cultural repression, racism, violence and exclusion of all kinds.

PART 8
Art Therapy

Art Therapy a Tool for Healing Process

Part of healing from a traumatic event is finding a way to allow its highly charged memory to be processed into normal memory, which somehow creates new meanings, behaviors, and outlooks. For some, healing occurs when the individual uses avoidance strategies to keep the traumatic memory inactivated until little by little it is accepted into the conscious narrative of one's life story. For other's active searches occur to find a new frame in which to place the traumatic memory in context of one's life that gives it meaning and acceptance rather than becoming overwhelming in grief, shame, fear and sorrow.

Memories from trauma are not integrated conceptually with other memories and are not available to be processed, worked through and continually transformed as are other aspects of our memories. A visual media may offer a unique means by which such traumatic images and memories are made accessible because of their graphic nature. Art therapy can provide an effective means of expressing, making meaning of, and at times transforming the resulting experiences of fear, loss, separation, instability and disruption.

Art's healing power is inseparable from its ability to transform the dark and terrible conditions of life into inspiring manifestations of the human spirit. The healing qualities of art is related to the total spectrum of the soul's experience and that art therapy application is dependent upon its willingness to meet new challenges and go to places where troubles in the human condition exist. Artistic expression inspires dignity and self-respect.

Even we are unable to control the most basic conditions of our lives, we are able to experience a liberating sense of freedom and expressive power in artistic activity . Nietzsche (1967) writes that unless we can do something creative with our pain, we are truly lost. He also stated that art is the great healer and the only force that is able "to turn these nauseous thoughts about the horror of absurdity of existence into notions with which one can live" (Nietzsche 1967 [1872], p60).

Jung (1966) also suggests that using imagery and drawing gave his patients a tool of not only talk about their inner experiences, but also doing something about it. He believes using art media to illustrate their inner images helps the individual to experience their dream or fantasy for second time, the person can study their image in all its parts and experience it completely. The person is encouraged to have an intellectual and emotional understanding of them. They must be consciously integrated, made intelligible, and morally assimilated. Jung in his book Man and his Symbols related the therapeutic process with archetypal symbolism in mythology and art. Jung valued the interpretation of arts by the patients which could bring about synthesis of personal and archetypal material. Symbolic events and images have a root in a collective origin, which has been experienced individually, with spiritual origins from the deepest unconscious sources.

In order to deal with painful events of fixed political or ethical positions, the hurt person may need to work creatively with the experience, maybe even relieve it in a creative way through the arts. The creative transformation of the wound therefore moves to the consciousness. Use of art in art therapy needs to be given the freedom to find its way to healing and this may involve perverse and disturbing expressions of darkness as well as light. According to Papadopoulos, labeling those who were exposed to these acts as "traumatized", and pathologizing them as victims, will distance the therapist and the person's experience and build a shield against the transformation of the devastating event. The art therapist functions as a guide to the process of creative transformation, as a companion who compassionately imagines the suffering of others, bears witness, shares the burden, and supports the repair.

Trauma inhibits the ability to symbolize, individuals may become stuck in a concrete mode of thinking, in the actual memory of the event or the recurring nightmare. They may be unable even to ask the questions. In this case, making meaning for them is very difficult, and the task of art therapy is to help individuals re-find a capacity for absorption and start to remember themselves as a whole (including sustaining memories), to differentiate past from present and restore their ability to symbolize. This is at times a long and painful process. If individuals are able to move from conscious reality and thinking into play, dream or creativity, they have a greater capacity to cope. This applies to both adults and children. The use of art therapy helps children who have been traumatized due to exposure to war. Art therapy transforms their traumatic experiences into creative power and prospects of healthy growth and development.

In Jung's view (1959), [the psyche is made of opposites; that is, any conscious attitude has its opposite in an unconscious one. These opposites manifest themselves in culture as well as in the psychological development of the individual. The collective unconscious is a layer in the psyche, which underlies the personal unconscious] (p3). The collective unconscious is the least accessible of the psyche material. The collective unconscious is expressed through archetypes, which are instinctual patterns which have no forms in their own right; they are not tangible, nor visible, but rather sense perceptions. They may constellate in dreams, myth and art (Jung, 1959).

Forms of unconscious, collective memory transmit trauma and grief through generations. Dokter conducted art therapy psychotherapy on Jewish clients who were not necessarily, nor in fact, directly affected by the Holocaust, and yet they carried the inter-generational scars. He believed that the reaction to the trauma of an experience which was both unthinkable and unspeakable took the form of repression on both a personal and collective scale. The medium of art psychotherapy offers a particular means of accessing and processing experiences which are otherwise not clear. In the cases of major trauma, art as a form of psychotherapy can be a helpful medium if used sensitively. It offers a means of working at a deep level and acknowledging and even sometimes integrating trauma. In the art the residual effect or even particular remembered incident can be externalized and be seen at a distance by the artist/client. In the picture these may be put outside for the first time. Subsequently there is a choice: of showing, disclosing and talking about the art. Sometimes through the art the individual can express unspeakable experiences without the need for words to describe the indescribable. The moving account of the need for, and benefits of, art psychotherapy in working with Holocaust survivors.

As addressed by McNiff (2005) Palestinian psychologists who worked with expressive art therapists from Israel reported that making art allows clients and the therapists to feel less impotent and more resourceful, when faced with overwhelming conditions of adversity. Arts are powerful tools of personal and community healing, and as history shows they are the most reliable source of soul repair and transformation when all other form of therapy are performed. People naturally respond to crisis in ways that focus on renewal, positive transformation and a deeper appreciation of life rather than the harmful effects of the event. The history of art and civilization, as well as our most personal experiences, show that difficult, painful and tragic occurrences often inspire humanity's greatest expressions and affirmations of life. He also explains that the overall sequence of experiences can be paradoxical and all too often cruel and in certain cases evil.

Creative expression can grow in the aftermath of a disaster or tragedy because it is the complete opposite of the trauma. Some people respond to the worst situation with affirmations of life and love for one another rather than sink deeper into a sense of hopelessness and victimization. Art therapists explored the role of the creative art therapy in the diagnosis and treatment of psychological trauma and discussed why the creative art therapy might be a treatment of choice. they worked with flash backs and nightmares and reproduced them by use of art. A visual media may offer a unique means by which such traumatic images and memories are made accessible because of their graphic nature.

Symbolic expression can be useful in relation to post traumatic stress disorder (PTSD). The way in which the art process and product enabled Vietnam Veterans to integrate their war experiences into their lives and gain mastery over the trauma even ten years after the event. The relieving of the event through the art making is perhaps necessary until some adequate resolution is found. By representing and objectifying it, Vietnam veterans could distance and defend themselves against the painful imprint without themselves being destroyed and therefore were able to gain more trust in their own overwhelming intensity that is formerly held (Golub, 1984).

During conducting art therapy in countries of political conflict, individuals expressed themselves differently through their arts, some drew or painted their horrific experiences, while many did not. Indeed, given the opportunity to make art in a refugee camp after war in Croatia in 1994, many of the children and adults drew landscape. These individuals may not have forgotten their experiences of war but seemed to instinctively choose not to graphically recall the details of the events they had lived through. Each individual has its own pace to allow their horrific images to unfold through art therapy, in contrary to the directive often given to children to directly draw their war experience (Kalmanowitz and Llyod, 2005). During art therapy with different populations in different countries with political conflict art therapists concluded that each individual would access or recall their traumatic experiences in different ways. Some had blurry memory, some had to detail narrative and some had bit and pieces of their memory. Many factors influence shaping traumatic memory such as levels of containment, physical and psychological safety, the time lapse from the traumatic experience, individuals' coping mechanisms and personal history.

Art therapists further affirm that conducting art therapy with refugee children and asylums helps the children to find solutions for dilemmas in an indirect way and become better equipped for their daily lives. In art therapy children can attach meaning to certain experiences without having to be clear. They can integrate their experiences at a conscious or unconscious level within their own system of meaning.

Art therapy prevention programs needs to be globally implemented, especially in countries hit by civil disturbances and/or by war, because they have the potential of helping young victims in a creative and meaningful way. Art therapy programs offer originality, acceptability, applicability, effectiveness and productivity. An aesthetic experience is transformational, and an aesthetic object seems to offer an experience where self-fragmentation will be integrated through a processing form. Even without verbal interpretation in art therapy, a transformation begins to take place in the inner world of the artist.

The use of metaphor puts us in touch with things that are not accessible in our conscious mind and we miss them out in our ordinary life. The creation of dynamic images take place in the space between the conscious and the unconscious. These creative images are more likely to occur spontaneously when we are relaxed. Working with the unconscious can be central in helping individuals unravel their internal responses to traumatic experiences. In addition to the art allowing for the unconscious to emerge, the image allows for the possibility to symbolize and perhaps disguise and this in itself may reveal that which is unspeakable.

At the heart of art therapy process is the ability of an individual to symbolize, imagine and be in touch with a range of emotions, which ends to different coping strategies. The actual physicality of making art allows for catharsis, expression and exploration. This connects with a key element of coping and resilience, namely, an active problem-solving approach to difficulties and stress.

Art Therapy and Cultural Sensitivity

For some cultures, one particular art form may be more central to tradition ways of coping than another. In the context of expressive art each different art form such as storytelling, drama, dance, music and fine arts has a powerful role to play. Being aware of cultural sensitivity is valid not only for art therapists working in cultures that are not their own, but also for art therapists working in their home country. In working with individuals from diverse cultures who have survived political violence, art therapists should be aware of their own beliefs about that culture, art therapist tools should be appropriate and indeed adequate.

Art therapists should consider the meaning of art in the culture they are working, and to find out what art has meant in the past, as well as the weight it carries in the present. The produced arts hold cultural, religious, political messages. People from different cultures have explicit and implicit attitudes towards art making and individual and societal expressions. Images may, in the same way as artifact or objects, hold symbolic meaning in which is implanted personal narrative or memory. During art making individuals draw not only on the personal unconscious but also on the collective unconscious or collective memories. It has been encouraged that individuals to work through the image to help reclaim a personal relationship to their rich cultural heritage.

Any form of ideology such as religious, political, or philosophical, reflect upon and integrate past and present personal experiences. For some individuals that, although the image making may serve to contain and even enable some emotional distance from their horrific experiences, it has been their belief system which has ultimately enabled them to survive and cope. Living through and surviving political violence can be an isolating experience. For many, the act of giving testimony and being witnessed is essential to making meaning. Sometimes in art therapy this story is told and heard through image.

For these individuals it is the telling that is essential to this activity. For many people being truly heard is all that is needed. Having the story seen or heard confirms that it did actually take place and that it is not, as the individuals may have begun to fear, in their imagination. Art can link individual's internal and external life and it has multiple meanings. They suggest that "if we use the arts in psychotherapy without taking into account their archetypal powers, and without making our clients aware or sensitive to this, that means we forget, one of the basic human instincts towards health and the sacred".

Some religious individuals attribute some meanings to their horrific life experiences by use of their religions. For other individuals who are not religious then searching for meaning may bring more questions than answers and yet individuals need to continue living and to cope with their new realities. For some individuals, their extreme experiences cannot be worked or understood or defined in linear terms. The art making during art therapy should facilitate and include multiple possibilities and provide the opportunity for multiple levels of narrative to unfold. Each person copes differently with extreme situations and remembers or forgets the events differently. They stated that people recover most effectively when they can integrate their experience into their belief system, but to do this they need to be able to recall their experiences, somehow draw them from their unconscious to conscious.

The use of Bilateral Art Therapy and Trauma Treatment:

The creative process of art making has been regarded as therapeutic in the field of art therapy and it has been considered as art in therapy and art as therapy. One of the art therapy approaches is bilateral stimulation of brain by use of left and right hand during creative process. Carole and McNamee report success in evoking new insights and positive benefits for their case study by use of Bilateral Art therapy Protocol.

The involvement of left and right brain during creation of visual art. Use of ATTP targets a specific traumatic memory provide the client with awareness of the somatic memory on the affective and emotional level. Talwar also asserts that the ATTP is a method that has an integrative approach offering a positive adaptive functioning model. The non-verbal core of traumatic memory can be accessed by use of ATTP approach. The ATTP approach has success in integrating the cognitive, emotional and physiological levels of trauma.

Conclusion

Witnessing a violent event involving death or life- threatening injury may redefine what constitutes a safe boundary for people. The trauma may shrink the self- boundaries between us and the outside world, threatening our survival. In childhood, witnessing a threat or injury to an individual will be understood as a threat to that child's own survival. Threats to the existence of our former caregivers remain a threat to us throughout adulthood as the meaning of those individuals to our survival always persists. The boundaries in childhood will remain undeveloped and under those circumstances, life may be perceived as a continuous painful and challenging experience.

It has been reported the periphery to exposure of traumatic event has a role into developing PTSD and phobic symptoms. It also has been discussed that despite the geographical location and distance from the exposure to political and religious violence, even through media, the witness is more likely to report anticipatory anxiety symptoms. To create space for expressing all sorts of thoughts is important for eliminating the breeding grounds for political extremism and Symbolizing is necessary in diminishing anxiety- driven behavior. It is also important to identify manipulation on the part of activists of groups of young, vulnerable traumatized victims in order to avoid the risks of escalation or a destructive spiral of revenge. From this perspective, we must be aware of the humiliating feelings being passed on from generation to generation, and what the consequences of that might be.

The overall conclusion of this literature review illuminates the idea that past traumatic experiences are not simply recovered memories in the usual sense of the word, but affects invading the present. Trauma linking and generational linking are two different tendencies that can dominate at different stages for each individual. The damage left in the wake of a war can be significant and enduring, even if the wounds are not visible. Combating the psychological aspects of a modern-day war can prove to be more immensely difficult than the physical aspects of war. If psychological aspects of war are left unaddressed, war will be a war that our children and our children's children will continue fighting.

PART 9
Healing Process and Methods

My healing process and tools

In-dwelling into my traumatizing past experiences inspired me to put two methods together to find access to my suppressed and repressed experiences related to living in Iran..

This research project utilized a qualitative, specifically Heuristic approach. Mustakas (1990) describes that "Heuristic inquiry is a process that begins with a question or problem which the researcher seeks to illuminate or answer. The question is one that has been a personal challenge and puzzlement in the search to understand one's self and the world in which one lives" (p15). The heuristic research approach helped me to have access to my deep rooted complex traumatic experiences to gain some insights that deepened my understanding of myself and also questions that have social and perhaps universal significance. Expressing tacit knowledge is possible through art and metaphor rather than word.

I used Art Therapy Protocol by Talwar to provoke challenges, and illuminate, rather than to confirm or secure knowledge. This research method enlarged perception, thoughts, and feelings in order to perceive slight relationships within complex wholes. It provided perception of new possibilities or originality that created new knowledge or transformed previous knowledge.

Heuristic research acknowledges the fundamental awareness that exists in the researcher's consciousness and provides an opportunity to receive the awareness and dwell on its nature and possible meaning. The heuristic research helps to find aspects that can be move from whole to parts and back to whole again, from individual to the general and back again, from experience to the concept and back again (Craig,1978, Cited at Mustakas 1990).

For the purpose of this study the research will afford the opportunity to discover how the art therapy process can facilitate my attempt to face the unresolved psychological struggle within due to exposure to human cruelty in the act of politics and religious violence that lead to symptoms of complex trauma.

Method

In the past I attempted to explore about my traumatic experiences and their effects on my psyche in talk therapy, but the verbal psychotherapy has failed. Talk therapy didn't relieve me from anxiety and the turmoil sensation that I used to feel in my chest and stomach when I talked or thought about Iran. The verbal account of a traumatic memory is not as important as the non-verbal memory of the fragmented sensory and emotional elements of the traumatic experiences. Talwar (2006) suggested a trauma art therapy protocol to integrate the cognitive, emotional and physiological levels of trauma by using both hands to stimulate right and left-brain hemispheres in the production of visual arts. Using both hands will stimulate left and right brain function which integrates both verbal and nonverbal processes. Using both hands would stimulate memories and experiences that reside in both sides of the brain". This process of creating facilitates the integration of experiences. By using this protocol, I have tried to put into pictures a speechless terror which I could not put into words. It is the trauma that is frozen in the somatic memory. The conducted research approach in this study is replicable but the finding and data are personal and unique and disallow to being duplicated.

Thirty-three art works are created in addition to a final work for the Creative Synthesis, following the specific heuristic protocol suggested by Mustakas (1990). All 33 paintings were produced during immersion. The arts have been painted in a series of 4-6 paintings each night for 7 consequent nights, following step by step recording and reflection in my journal.

Gathering of Data

While collecting data associated with the long-term traumatic exposure of violence and cruelty related to religious and political conflict, I realized my memories of those events were disorganized. In order to access those memories and determine the emotional significance of each experience I set up strict time-lines and limitations for the immersion process. I gathered data over the course of seven consecutive nights and dedicated the immersion process to specific ages (14-27) and memories during that time. The data consists of journal entries and writing about thoughts and emotions prior, during, and post the art making process of each night.

The data collected consists of the research and documentation of the following:

In first night: Considered age: 14 years of age. I create four paintings that examined the traumatic experiences surrounding my exposure to the fundamentalist extremist Islamic revolution of Iran.

Second night: Considered age: 15 years of age. I created four paintings exploring memories related to witnessing executions, assassinations, and deaths of friends and family members. This happened post revolution with the change of regime to the Islamic Republic.

Third night: Considered age: 15 years of age. I created six paintings exploring the period of time in which the Islamic government ordered women to cover their hair and body while in public. Women who disobeyed were subjected to brutal punishments that included torture, arrest and even death.

The forth night: Considered ages: 15-24 years of age. I created six pieces of art that explored the trauma associated with the eight years of war that took place between Iraq and Iran one year after the revolution. During this time of my life, I was exposed to fear, death, danger, grief, mourning, pain and suffering.

The fifth night: Considered age: 14- 20 years of age. I created four pieces of arts to explore the trauma associated with bombing and death. During this period, I was exposed to destruction, death, and horrific scenes of human cruelty instigated by politics and terrorism. Bombings became a consistent part of public life and instilled overwhelming fear and anxiety in civilians.

The sixth night: Considered Age: 21-27years of age. I created four paintings that explored my scattered and traumatic memories experienced during this time. These experiences included but are not limited to memories of being arrested by the Islamic police for no specific reason and being forced as a midwifery student to take care of soldiers wounded by chemical bombings and radiation. I call this night a residual night.

The seventh night: Considered age: 44 years of age. I feel a strong urge to dedicate this night to my experience as a witness to the Green Wave Riot in Iran (2009). This uprising relates to police brutality, corruption, the lack of free election and freedom of speech as well as economic issues related to high rates of unemployment and food price inflation. I am exposed, once again, to the rage, torture, and death of war, up-close, from my home in the United States via the media. Observing the coverage opened up old scars, made them ooze and triggered my PTSD symptoms. Four paintings are created on this night.

The exploration of the literature was not completed until after the immersion phase, which is unlike many studies. As McNiff (2005) suggests, "in art based studies connections to literature are often made after inquiry is complete. "Review literature after the project is complete minimizes bias and helps to encourage the research to create arts with no external influences.

Material and procedures in this method followed the protocol designed by Talwar (2006). The procedures are as follows, a large sheet (22" X29") of Bristol board is taped on the wall. The paints are set up on the other side of the room in the opposite direction of the paper about 7 feet apart. The work place permits the full body movements, the tempera paints are laid out in open jars on a table in a variety of colors ranging through a continuum from white to black. The space allows me to walk back and forth between the paper and the paints. The walking process encourages dual processing or bilateral stimulation. Other art material such as charcoal and pastels are laid on the table next to the paints to provide free choice with minimum limitation of use of material. Before each painting I write about a memory of traumatic event, presenting the facts and events of the memory. I explored each traumatic experience related to the period of my life and I continued painting related to that experience until I felt no emotional disturbances at recall of that specific memory. Six sessions are planned however they can be expanded if necessary.

The rest of the approach follows the instructions by Moustakas (1990) which includes 8 days of incubation and the next steps are the Illumination and Explication and finally Creative Synthesis, which step by step I walk you through them to help you understand and learn the process for your future use.

Incubation phase:

During this period, I disengaged myself from the creative process. I set aside my artwork for 10 days and organized activities with my family. As Moustakas suggests, distancing myself from the process is essential for "silent nourishment, to create awareness of some dimension of phenomena or creative integration of it's parts or qualities". I engaged in my daily routine of parenting.

Analysis of Data

In the heuristic process there are two distinct analysis explorations that are called illumination and explication. They serve to allow for a revisiting of the data to gain insights and then achieve a depth of understanding in the explication of the analysis.

Illumination:

During this period, I reunited myself with the arts I produced during the immersion phase. I began by studying each group of art created on its specific night. I searched for themes, images, thoughts and feelings that I hadn't already acknowledged and explored during the immersion process. I carefully considered and studied the use of space, lines, tension, choice of color, and shapes in each painting. I also looked for emerged themes that could potentially provide more answers and explanations for specific experiences. I was open to a new state of awareness.

I searched for relevant meaning in the uncovered and repressed artistic material produced during the immersion phase. Then, I read the journals that accompanied each piece on its specific night. I dialogued with the art pieces that still held residual emotions and took note of them in my journal. After viewing each series, I brought them to my therapist to explore and investigate new meanings, questions and unresolved processing. Each new and significant insight was carefully noted.

Explication:

During this phase I began inspecting relevant literature to the topics I addressed in my immersion process. I chose to gather literature in this stage to ensure that the research wouldn't influence my psychological reactions to the exposed trauma of my past. Studying relevant articles in the initiation phase could have influence my emotional reactions and cause confusion and doubt in regard to the authenticity of my own feelings. After gathering all the information, I integrated my own collected data and discovered new meanings in the process. After gathering all the information, my data was presented, and new meanings were recognized. Moustakas explains that "purpose of the explication phase is to fully examine what has awakened in consciousness, in order to understand its various layers of, meanings".

Creative Synthesis:

After I familiarized myself with all the data in its major components, qualities, and themes and the meaning and details of the experience as a whole. I used my tacit and intuitive powers and self-searching to create a final culminating piece of art. The art addresses the core themes of the undertaken research including the art therapy method (ATTP) and its therapeutic effect on my psyche.

PART 10
Immersion, revisiting and re-experiencing

The arts have been gathered using a systemic process in conjunction with the inherent and therapeutic effects of art- making. The data comprises the art created, textual witnessing and processing outlined in the design of the study. The paintings produced were utilized in the conceptualization and exploration of unresolved anger, loss, grief, fears and emotions. The artistic process provided me the mental space to engage some of the most frightening aspects of my history. I carefully noted the feelings and insights that arose during the production of art, which varied from aggression to sublimation, through an uncritical manner and without the fear of destruction of self or others. I proceeded to carefully review the art myself and, at times, with my therapist, to record all observations, feelings, emerged themes and symbols.

First Night, Revolution

Journal entry; "I am 14 years old and recently completed my first year of high school. Adolescence for me is like stepping off an edge and falling into the most beautiful world, one full of music, fun, and enlightening education. The riots break out near the end of my first year of high school. People are angry and aggressive, and chaos unfolds everywhere. Many of us are faced with complications attributable to the strikes. At times we live without transportation, electricity, and gas, even in the hospitals. At home, my mother and father worry. We listen to the BBC day and night, and the news grows more and more horrific. Anxiety perpetuates our society as political strife turns to turmoil. Movie theatres filled with people are burnt to ashes and banks and governmental offices are under attack. People fear going to work, as so many of them are attacked by extremists. My father urges my sisters and I do not get involved in any political group. He is a general in Shah's military and we fear for his life. Every day we question, 'Will they arrest him? Will he be killed?' Danger is prevalent and a prominent part of our consciousness. My sisters and I listen as our parents speak in whispers to family and friends. In high school, many of the teenagers are active participants in various political groups but seem unaware of the developing violence. They are more preoccupied with enjoying the autonomy they've gained in the midst of all the chaos. They perceive the revolution in the same way they perceive action movies. My father is in danger and we live under a cloak of fear. My mother is scared and anxious, our future is uncertain.

As the heat rises in Iran, so do the screaming protestors, and they are quickly approaching the military community in which we live. Supporters of Khomaynee, the leader of the Islamic sector of the revolution, consistently target citizens with religious propaganda. The electricity goes out as our world falls into a state of terror.

The core sensations I experience at this time by re-emerging these memories stem from fear. By remembering these I feel my lower back aches, there are knots in my stomach and I am exhausted. As remembering the assassination attempt on my father, amplify these feelings. Luckily, he isn't in his office at the time. I am terrified, I feared losing him in the past to illness, but the reality of the attempt brings that fear even closer.

At night, the sickly-sweet smell of burnt wood and plastic permeates the air while the screams of our neighbors interrupt the silence. My family lives in a military community. Because we are considered friends of Pahlavie's regime, the momentum of the revolution threatens us. Soldiers stand on top of our roofs for protection.

Most people are turning against Shah and he leaves the country as the riots worsen. His departure has left those of us who have remained loyal to his regime hopeless and in shock. Our society drops into a state of chaos. Terrorists roam the streets and many people of all political beliefs are killed. It feels as though the devil rules our country as Khomaynee gains power. People I know are being arrested and executed so often, it becomes familiar. Some of students at my school are arrested and killed by the regime. They were 16 years old. Teenaged Gun Sepahi, a group of soldiers who enforce the regime, are given the authority to search citizens at will and kill when necessary. My friend's father is murdered. Images of dead bodies are shown on the front page of the newspapers, and my recollection of their faces remains crystal clear long after I turn the page. The glory and respect of our country is dying, and the prime minister has just been prosecuted and killed.

One night, the possibility of an attack on our home leads us to flee to a relative's. When we return, our windows are shattered, and bullet holes line the walls of our neighbor's house. Our country is a mess. Innocent people are being killed every day. Children lose their fathers, and I hear mother's screaming in anguish. All I can do is listen to their cries. I am tormented by the blood, injustice and visceral death caused by this revolution. The world in which I live is colored in black. My family doesn't know whom to trust.

My father resigned from his position at military, the job that he loved and was proud of, and stays inside, listening to the news. Every day we hear of more deaths, most of them are his friends and colleagues. He sinks into a depression and becomes increasingly withdrawn as he mourns the losses of those he cared for. We worry for him as his health deteriorates. He's losing weight and I fear he can't handle much more. My mother is strong. She stands for what she believes in, liberal and smart, she fights for her rights. She is the one capable of saving us. My sisters and I stay at home or at the homes of very close friends.

At this point, I find relief only in my family and friends. We remain close and supportive, finding solace in shared turmoil. There is nothing more tangible than the bonds of our love. We share our pain and in doing so, lessen the burdens of trauma. I still fear the people fighting for the revolution. I hold them in contempt, in disrespect. My feelings vacillate between extreme rage and shock. I still experience numbing, sadness, anxiety and fear."

I realized I can't write anymore, and I stopped and looked at the room, and all the art materials and white paper on the wall, it felt like the energy of the memory is making me to move forward to express and put it all out of my system. I walked to the paints and looked at the colors at this point I just allowed my visual expression to take me. I used my right hand to express what is in my psyche with full trust that this can be it, the opportunity and the window that I was waiting for to open up and let out all the dark memories. I had a little bit of anticipation and fear of stepping down but I knew based on my education and experience that art is the solution and I am willing to face the pain and let it out. This kind of exploration appears like a surgery that there is no tranquilizers involved, it feels like ancient Indian tribal rituals to free the soul by going through painful physical and emotional pains. I was ready to face them all.

I started painting with my right hand: During the creative process, I relived memories and emotions experienced during the revolution. My chest felt heavy, as though bricks were compressing my heart. My thoughts were dark and full of fear. I hated feeling this way. In the painting, a black vortex sits in the air, a drop of dark rain falls. I can witness again in my painting that People are suffering but this time manifested in the midst of purple movement. They are being killed. Those dark shapes at the top are safe, but the ones in the middle are dying. The dead rest on the purple side of the painting. It reminds me of a tsunami, dark and unrelenting.

At this point I feel hopeless and helpless. I feel worthless, powerless, and scared. I am a mess.

"Image 1, Revolution"

After expressing the painful emotional and mental memories of revolution and creating the first piece, I felt a painful urge to continue painting as there is more to come out, I walked to the paint colors on the table and with left hand picked up a brush, at this point I just follow my body and my sensations to do whatever they like to do, I was an observer and allowing the surfacing of dark and painful memory to occur. My chest was heavy as I began to paint. Feelings of hopelessness and fear surrounded me. I used a soft brush as the bristles pick up more paint and create smooth strokes without pressure, as I had no energy to press the brush on the paper, my hand was working as it was a vent or the only way or outlet to let the pain suffice. When I was close to being done, I splashed some paint on the painting. The kinetic movement was comforting and repelling.

"Image 2, Revolution"

I experienced feelings of deep hopelessness as I created this piece. The painting appears to be divided in the middle of the page; a frame contains the images representing the disturbing emotions experienced. On the left side of the piece, I see a shape holding something small; I think it is a monkey, being fed from the red breast of a headless body. A dog sits on her hind legs, her front feet wave in the air, and her ears are down as though she is afraid. There is another creature in front of the dog, and although its back is turned away from her, evil thorns point in her direction. The creature is watchful, alert and disappointed in the dog. A line divides the two of them, but they seem to be connected anyway. Also, in the painting is "Mola", disguised as an old woman, he carries a stick and looks down at the dog. A black creature whisper to the Mola. Other entities surround this relationship. This piece is full of dark colors, negative energy and many emotions.

I realized I am not done with the process and I have the urge to continue, I used right hand, at this point it appeared my right and left hands are taking turns to have a dialog with one another, like two very close friends who have reunited after so many years after thirty years of losing each other's, they couldn't wait to share their painful and confusing experiences with one another, it was such uniting after the death of loved one, it felt like a resurrection of death for two very close friends to help and share with one another what was like to be there and to witness all of those painful memories.

I continued the 3rd painting with right hand: In this painting I used blue, the color of rain water, to wash the canvas. After putting the blue paint on the paper then I found the courage to draw guns, blood, dead bodies, and to display the trauma of my surroundings, the consequences of war and it's cruelty against humanity. The blue color made me feel safe enough to illustrate the dark memories that encompassed my reality. The painting, itself, seems to

"Image 3, Revolution"

scream. Red tears slide down the blue canvas. Everyone is hurt and in a state of pain. There is a girl covering her face in fear, crying blood for all those lost to hideous crimes. She hides her face from the bodies of innocent children, mothers, and fathers. She is me and the tears are mine. I have a strong desire to finish this painting. I feel as though I owe this piece of art to my people. I need to expose these atrocities. The painting is a representation of trauma. Innocent people lie in pools of their own blood and a deep river runs through the canvas, connecting us all. Hand is above my head, spreading injustice. People have been manipulated, hypnotized, and controlled, ignorant people whose ridiculous beliefs kept them blind from the truth. They condoned the war and executions for a seat in heaven. They believed in empty promises from Islamic leaders. I watch the river of blood flow, and I tell Khomaynee and his followers to stop. The stop signs dripping with human blood are everywhere. Stop killing, stop, STOP.

I started walking toward paint and continued with left hand:

"Image 4, Revolution"

This final piece is sacred. It is white and peaceful. My left hand chose to use a round brush instead of the square, pointed one and proceeded to saturate its bristles in white paint. I covered the wet red with white and created pink, the color of love and compassion. There is a softer fluency to this painting, a rhythmic harmony within its story. The canvas is covered in thick, white brush Strokes. The orange paint on the picture came last. I used it to create warmth and gentle movement. The thickness of paint is amazing; it holds so many contained emotions.

As I painted, I longed to detach from the process. The sensations of trauma stirred within me and I felt slightly overwhelmed. I forced myself to continue and used the sensations to paint. While I painted with white, visions of ghosts moved gently across the canvas in thick strokes. I noticed there was a bit of red paint on the brush. The red represented blood and as I continued to paint in white, the red blood gently washed away.

A black-out in Santa Monica interrupts my process and I'm left in a black hole of emotion. The first thought crossed my mind was, no way, universe is playing with me. I felt heavy and began to recall memories of the revolution and war. The lights would go out, and we would anticipate the sirens indicative of the bombardment that would follow. I needed to bring myself back to the present, to remind myself that I was safe. I used my lap-top as a flashlight and left the room, I couldn't stay by myself in that room, it was like the room was the past and I was so scared to stay there. I ran to my bedroom and found my sleeping husband. I looked at the clock. It was 11:44pm. I am no longer scared; I actually feel protected. The dark spirits that invaded my heart for so long are gone. The shadows of death, confusion and fear don't haunt me as they used to. I found my way out of the darkness, and though I won't go to sleep until the lights turn back on, I feel more relief than anything else. I went to check on my kids, and as I watched them I am reminded to stay strong, I need to stay in control. I think about my family sleeping and I think about the families that slept during the revolution. So many of them were killed unexpectedly. Were they ready for it? Were they ready to be killed so brutally? They had kids; they must have been so scared, not knowing what would happen to their families after they died. I wonder what their last thoughts were before the execution, how their children processed their grief. How could they ever forgive or forget? I imagine how unbearably painful that must have been. I wonder who helped them. So many innocent people died. What was the revolution for? Money? Power? There was never an intention to honor humanity or spirituality. The revolutionists fought for their own animalistic gratification. Husbands were executed and their wives were manipulated into sleeping with the Molas (Islamic represent or and religious leaders). Those in power always had ways to make the coins fall on their behalf. I think back and know my mother, my sisters, and I were in danger. The black-out allowed me to make a different association with unexpected darkness. At first, I was drawn into the panicked memories of the revolution. To prevent myself from being sucked into the vortex of fear I reminded myself that I couldn't lose control. If I panicked, I would sink into a dark abyss. If I stayed in control, if I stayed strong, I could handle anything. I took a moment to look outside. It was dead dark, and I saw nothing, no monsters or victims. I used to hear the sounds of the revolution all the time. I don't anymore. The threat is gone. I am safe and at home in the United States. Nobody is coming to scare or hurt me, or my family. I feel strong and empowered. I am reminded of the fighter I've always been, of the woman who remained in control during the most difficult times of my life living with Islamic regime in Iran. I remember my capacity to survive in the face of all the adversity I've encountered. I am done with this process. I can still recall the shouts of the revolution, but I don't feel scared. My family is safe.

Second Night, War Between Iran and Iraq

Significant ages: 15-24 years. The following paintings were gathered on the second night of the immersion process. The traumatic memories and emotions experienced are in relation to the war. Once again, I began journaling to stimulate thoughts and memories before delving into the artistic process:

"I am 15 years old. It is summer and the war between Iraq and Iran has started. Tension pervades the streets as new restrictions are enforced. The government has recently announced that all women must wear uniforms with veils if they wish to go out in public. It feels like a cruel joke, and collectively, we are in disbelief.

When Iraq invaded Iran, my family and I are residing in the capital. Gas and food have become expensive commodities and my family feels the stress of the shifting economy. The new government has cut my father's salary and both he and my mother worry about finances. The universities have closed down; the new government is revolutionizing the education system. Young men are called to war; most of them are just 18 years old.

At this time, any young man caught walking down the street is stopped by the police and sent immediately to serve in military and into combat. People have taken to hiding their children away to prevent them from being drafted. Everywhere I go, I hear talks about boys being sent into the military.

The new government has taken control of the media, and the television and radio spew propaganda about the rewards of war. Young boys are told that in exchange for signing up to fight in the war, they will be given the key to heaven. Most of these promotions are spoken of in schools to under aged boys. Families feel as though death is breathing down all of their necks, we fear for each other. Among those called to war are brothers and fathers of those I love. My first boyfriend is recruited and killed. I witness mothers crying the names of their lost son's; their grief is a burning fire of sorrow. Everywhere I look, women are in mourning. My next-door neighbor's husband is executed, and my friend loses her father. Their screams blanket the air and break my heart.

The people of my city are pale, depressed, and scared. My friends and I sometimes sit together, saying nothing; we witness the devastation and darkness in silence.

The economy worsens, and citizens are forced to line up on the street for food and gas. Islamic fundamentalist fanatics are brutally burglarizing, hanging and killing innocent people. They sell the dead bodies of the loved ones to their families. Everywhere I go, I see death. My mother's cousins are killed in the war, and she worries incessantly for my father's safety. A funeral is held in every family. Everyone I know has lost someone they loved. In search of comfort, some run toward religion, to the teachings of the Quran. Others run the opposite direction, away from religion and turn against Islam. I ran toward the hatred of war, religion and Islam.

As I attempted to pick up the brush and letting go of resistance to visually express my feelings and memories, a huge surge of sadness took over my body and I started crying, the whole process of this art was accompanied with my tears, I cried throughout the creation of this piece. I am sad; the loss of life during this time in the revolution weighs heavily on me. I visualize wives, mothers and children crying, they are deeply heartbroken. Their eyes bleed as they hold the graves of their sons and husbands in their hands. I think about my mother, who lost two of her cousins, the ones who saved my father's life after the revolution.

In the painting, everyone is dressed in black. In the shadow of the Quran are the painted words, "az khoone javanane vatan laleh damideh", the English translation of that phrase: 'from country youth's blood tulips are growing". Tulips are growing in the shade of Quran; it is the book written with blood. And the tulips are grown in the field of hatred, hell not heaven.

The amount of suffering in our community at this time is tremendous. People are dying in the name of God. Young men are used to diffuse bombs and land mines; they are being slaughtered by the people they have put their faith in betrayal.

"Image 5, War"

The soldiers that do make it back come home with severe psychological symptoms. I am feeling extremely sad as I paint. I feel empty and helpless next to the shock of these memories. I am mute and can't speak for the moment. My throat feels so tight and my jaw and ears are heavy. I understand what's going on and I know I can handle it. I am scared, but in control. I feel the heaviness of my jaw and throat sink down into my chest and heart. I can feel the pain and tension move.

"Image 6, War"

I am still crying during the creation of Image 6. The heaviness in my jaw and chest is still present. I look at the ghost like dark figures spiraling down through the vortex of death. The painful emotional experience leads me to continue painting and switch to right hands. At this points my hands are having the dialog and take turns. It seems there is no energy left for mental processing and putting this painting into words.

"Image 7, War"

Image 7 illustrates the bombardment of civilians as they run toward the basement for protection. I am angry, enraged. I feel fiercely protective and strong; I will kill to save my life. I quickly switch to left hand, it seems with continuing the process I am looking for a venue, or relief.

I continued the process by switching my hand to left and started painting Image 8,

The strokes in red may represent my anger, but I didn't apply very much pressure with the brush. The red glided smoothly across the canvas, which might suggest that, while I was angry, I was also calm. From another point of view, I could have been too scared to express my emotions completely. As I painted, the heaviness in my throat kept me from feeling like I wanted to speak. There is a drop of blood in the middle of the canvas. It looks shapeless. The red lines in the painting remind me of bombings. They seem to be attacking each other, nothing seems fit.

"Image 8, War"

I still felt like I need to continue the process, as if my mind is searching for an answer, I switched to right hand to create Image 9. I am the woman in the painting. I am sitting. There is something heavy and black stuck in my throat; it's moving down my neck toward my heart. A black and white monster's head is hanging in front of me. His nose drips with snot on my hand that is pointing to injustice. There is another head underneath the monster's head, this head is missing a brain. I am pointing my left hand at the emptiness inside his head. I am illustrating the ignorance of the Islamic war. There isn't any reason or logic that can support or condone this kind of violence or cruelty. I have something unpleasant dripping down my head, it bothers me, and at a certain point I consider cleaning it off the painting. I decide to leave it. I have thorns sticking out of my back, like wings. I can't fly with them; perhaps I have them to scare the enemy.

In this painting I am facing my fears; I am facing the devil. The energy of this piece is dark. The ground I sit upon is full of thorns. They hurt my feet, but I stand my ground. I keep my eyes and hand focused on the monster. I feel the pain and heaviness of my surroundings, but I am not afraid. The monster and I are negotiating; I am trying to show him the error of his ways.

I glance over the paint jar that I mixed the paints I used for this piece, it seemed to speak to me as I mixed them into the desired colors. They took the shape of a girl, holding her legs to her chest; her head rests on her knees. She is crying. An injured fox is making it's way to her. Underneath them is something sticky and black, something disgusting

"Image 9, War"

I felt an urge to play with paints by pouring white paint in a clean paint jar, I let the process take me to what it wanted to create, then I poured red paint into white paint. The red color penetrated the center of white paint and left a small red hole like a bullet mark, it felt the white has been shot at, and then the red paint seeped out from underneath the body of white, to the sides. It appeared as though the white paint was bleeding.

"Image 10, War"

To my surprise I saw the reenactment of the scene I saw on news, I am reminded of "Neda". During the 2009 riot in Iran, an Iranian woman's murder was caught on tape, the camera rolled as her life left her body. The media replayed that reel over and over again. That woman's name was Neda, and her tragic death and image is present with me as I continue to mix these paints. Her image has always haunted me.

The white in this mixture of paint represents the innocence of the young people, caught in the turmoil and chaos of war. The red represents their blood, so casually spilled. As I witness this creation, my throat is tight. I see myself in the face of a cloaked figure. She is wearing bloody clothes and carries the heaviness I feel in my throat. Looking deeply into her face, I notice a growing tree. I believe it represents the expanding understanding I've gathered during the production of this thesis.

After mixing the white and red, I began creating another combination of colors. This time, I choose white and yellow. When I poured the yellow in the new paint jar Image 11 formed. I saw a young girl, curled up into a ball, her knees tucked into her chest. The girl is another representation of me. On my back is a face, its' mouth is wide open and ugly. It's speaks to me, but I don't understand what is said. I then proceed to my surprise I notice a green dot of paint next to her head. I visualize a green wave, which symbolizes the deep sadness I feel toward the Islamic Republic of Iran, and the injustice and crime that persists there to this Day.

The last step in the completion of this piece was to gently coat the canvas with a few white and yellow brush strokes. These colors were particularly healing for me. Each brush stroke soothed an aching scar like a healing cream. The tension in my throat subsided as I continued to paint.

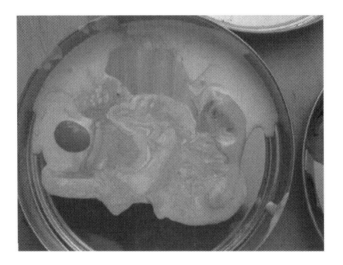

"Image 11, War"

I started painting with my left hand creating Image 12, as the war tensions have left my body, I started choosing brighter colors, immediately I realized that these colors do not have a place in the war. When I look at the green in this painting now, I see the sun, life, and healing that has been a long time coming. I have no urge to continue as if I have processed all the unresolved materials related to war.

"Image 12, War"

As I cleaned up after the completion of the final painting, I catch a glimpse of myself in the mirror. I look exhausted, as though I have just come out of a bombardment. I have red and black paint all over my face, the colors that symbolized sorrow and blood. I will rest now.

Third Night (Women's Rights)

I am 16 years old. It feels like it's a crime to be a woman living under the fanatic fundamentalist Islamic regime. We are forced to wear uniforms and veils whenever we go out in public. We bear the uncomfortable scarves, long sleeves, and cover coats, even in the sweltering months of summer. The consequences for not abiding these restrictions are severe; if even a little bit of our hair shows, we are treated like criminals. Women are insulted, assaulted and sometimes raped and killed by the ignorant, impoverished men that act as law enforcers. There are no consequences for these crimes and many of these men capitalize and exploit the power they have over our gender.

I feel like I have my life cradled, protectively in the palm of my hand. If I were to drop it, out of neglect or in a moment of pleasant distraction, I could lose it and no one would be able to help me. That is what life is like at this time. As women, we have to be constantly aware of our surroundings. We are always in danger.

Women are kidnapped from the cars of their husbands, from their homes, and houses of friends. The law enforces can arrest anyone they want to, without reason or cause. Their power is unlimited.

I am afraid to walk down the street under influence of this fanatic oppressive government. Every time I venture out, I take precautions to ensure my appearance doesn't provoke attention; I make sure my hair is tucked in, and my skin doesn't glow. My expression must always be angry. At this point under this situation, women are the main targets of violence and cruelty. Living here is like walking through a dark and horrific jungle every day; you must walk consciously and carefully, because if you don't, you are sure to be eaten by a wild animal."

At this point I stopped writing in my journal, and I was ready to use creative process to express my inner pain related to injustice and many years of abuse on women.

I started painting the image 13, with my right hand. A girl stands in the center of this painting. She is a representation of me, green as the young plant and alive. She dares to dream as she faces the hardships of the world head-on. For now, she is faceless, searching to define her identity. Yellow blankets the space surrounding her and illuminates her chest. This represents hope or strength. Yellow is also the color of the solar plexus chakra. The pointy brown lines that stretch across the canvas represent the trauma caused by the attacks to her personal freedom and physical and emotional safety. She must cope with the stress of these lines every day. At times, it suffocates her.

Two black, domineering figures invade her space. They want to control her, get inside of her mind. They represent the female police of Islam. They are cruel women, dangerous and violent. The supreme leaders of the government, the Molas, Khomaynee and Khameneyee, support them. They do whatever they wish. The girl can't escape them.

The supreme leader hovers over the policewomen; he keeps them in place by sticking sharp nails up their asses. He appears as Dracula, and they are his previous victims, transformed into vampires that fight for his regime.

In this piece, the supreme leader is a Mola; all of his extremities have been turned into penises.

"Image 13, Women's Right"

Everything at this time revolves around sex, objectification and exploitation. The government denounces women, proclaiming they provoke men into committing sin. A Quran is painted in the top, left-hand corner of the canvas. On one side of the page there are excerpts on violence and cruelty, on the other, the rules of sex have been written. The Molas drink in the essence of those pages, using them as fuel to exploit more women. They believe they are the protectors of Islam, to them; women are commodities and easily sacrificed. The girl's humanity, sanity, dreams, and youth are crushed under the pressure of the Molas penis.

I look at this visual expression and feel helpless and scared. I feel hateful, disgusted and enraged. I feel it in my hands, my stomach. My shoulder tingles with the sensations of discomfort and my jaw is tight.

Now I felt I have to switch hands and start painting with left hand, I began painting Image 14, feeling strong, but started to cry in the middle of the process. I cry so hard, my head aches, and I can't seem to stop. I am releasing so much tension. I cry for women, for all the ones that are raped, killed, held captive, and stoned; for all the women that are in pain, and alone with their fear and grief. I continue to cry as the pain and pressure in my forehead worsens. It appears that I am releasing so much pain and sorrow from collective consciousness of abused women, as a woman we are deeply connected with all the female energy in the world and in face of cruelty or abuse of women we feel their pain rising from our deepest being.

What is this ugly, brown, shapeless painting about? Who brought upon this sorrow? It is so hard for me to look at this painting. It is a self- portrait of an Iranian woman. A woman who has been assaulted, belittled, and invaded over and over again. I am so sad. This portrait is a representation of the many beautiful, intelligent women of Iran that continue to suffer. It represents me. I imagine the women that are held in the prisons, being raped and stoned over and over again. God stop the injustice! As one of my clients said, "If I believed in God, I would be very angry at him."

"Image 14, Women's Right"

I started painting with right hand (image 15), at this point I feel my hands are working at a time guiding by an invisible force. I feel as soon as I provided the safety and platform for visual expression the creative process is taking charge and step by step working through the unresolved traumatic materials. I continue the process, Image 15 is a representation of me. I am wearing a long coat and a thick veil; this is a uniform that has been mandated from government for women to wear. I look like a shocked mummy, buried in depression.

"Image 15, Women's Right"

Using my left hand, I am painting Image 16, this painting allowed me to breathe. I began by taking a few deep breaths, which helped to liberate the tension and pressure living within my chest. I see birds in this painting, two of them. I see water and waves. The birds appear to be free but look towards a formless shape in the mountains. It is a snake, warning against the darkness in the middle of the painting.

The movement of the birds is mystical, but one of them, the one in back, seem to be trapped by black lines. They are trapped in the cultural chaos of Islam, and they need help. Will they ever be free? What are they saying to one another? The top bird says, "I can't bare this dark line around my head, I can't take it!"

Another bird responds, "We will grow stronger wings and fly, be patient."

There is a scar on the head of one of the birds. She is in pain and needs to be healed. I feel relief, and freer upon the completion of this painting.

"Image 16, Women's Right"

In image 17 created by right hand, a woman comes to the rescue in this painting. She is green, strong, healthy and powerful. The pink represents the power of love. The deliberate splashes of green don't necessarily

"Image 17, Women's Right"

compliment the pink, but it does illustrate the effort it takes to stand in love; to fight with everything you have and survive in the face of injustice. The figure is a cry for help to have a face of courage, ready to spread love despite all the atrocities, but it still seems just as an attempt, a wish for strength to survive.

In image 18 created by left hand, I feel free, loose, and healthy. Pieces of me are scattered throughout the painting. It is a reflection of my love. An angel holds me in the top left corner. My angel is hardworking, powerful, and reliable; she is dedicated to the job assigned to her. I feel empowered and healthy in my identity. The green in this painting represents a woman, who floats above the pain.

Orange colors the canvas, representing the currency of life. There is a small imperfection

in the left corner. It is a scar from my past. It allows me to be conscious of the pain and turmoil I've survived. If I kiss those imperfections rather than reject them, I feel better. The lips in the painting represent those kisses.

I let go of the woman who is pleasant, but insincere. The beauty of my character is in the truth of both my present and past.

Something rests on bottom of this painting; it might be a mouse. A dragon stands unsteadily in the right corner; it is another one of my imperfections. Accepting my imperfections is hard, but they are undeniable parts of me.

What are those things on the ground? The one in front wants to build an underground tunnel, and escape from the trauma. She believes she can run away from her pain, from her past. She doesn't want the angel to catch her. The angel watches this unfold, and knows there is no escape. This is my consciousness, telling me that, in order to truly heal, I must face the truth. The other thing on the ground has something on her back; maybe it's a wing, maybe it is turning to a bird to escape. The pains in my jaw and stomach have dissipated. I feel free.

"Image 18, Women's Right"

Fourth Night, (Bombing)

Journal writing, "I remember applying to university and being denied. Despite my good grades, the enrollment committee refused to consider me because I was reported of not being able to cover my hair properly. I was told I didn't measure up to the requirements for Islamic students. I had to go through so much mental suffering and one year of fighting for my right and beg and ask for mercy and find connections to allow me to sit for exam the year after while covering my hair properly, to find a possible chance of re-admission. I remember I was able to get a meeting with the head of admission of universities which was an uneducated mola, in our meeting he told me that he knows who I am since I am one of the twelves students who got admitted to medicine but they don't know what to do with us. He explained that the allegations against us is not strong enough to deprive us from furthering our education but at the same time we are not a good fit to get into university, based on the Islamic measurement. Despite my high academic performances since I never joined the prayer group I was prevented and deprived from pursuing my dream. Despite my admission at medicine they didn't let me get in. I was so sad and angry when I found out how my future and destiny is a joke to others. It was unreasonable and unacceptable but what could I do, I had to comply and with the world of sadness walk away. They didn't let me in to medical school. I didn't give up and I took the next year university exam again, with the hope this time some miracle happens and they let me in. I did very well in the entry exam and this time my admission letter reported that, midwifery has been chosen for me since the school was unisex and was a better fit for me who fail to cover my hair properly. They also did a twist in my admission that I won't be able to sit for any other entry exams. If I wanted to go to university the only thing I could study was midwifery and that is all. This was the biggest defeat for me, I couldn't believe that I didn't have any control over my future career and education. I didn't have money or resources at that time to leave Iran. The country was involved with 8 years' war and during this turmoil no one wanted to leave the loved one and family behind. Also, there were so many negative stories about Iranian students overseas who were not been treated kindly, due to the act of Islamic revolutionary committee, taking hostage in American embassy employees who supposed to have national amenity. To the world's eye all Iranians were bunch of uncontrollable savages and terrorists. It appears there is not much place for any Iranian in the world.

While attending Tehran University, I was exposed to many traumatic situations. After the bombardment, chaos reigned. one day I stumbled upon the remains of human body parts due to civilian bombing activity. It was awful seeing my country in ruins, homes were demolished after street bombings and many people I cared about were suffering. Soldiers who survived the chemical bombings came home with lifelong problems. I looked at them in pity, lamenting that they didn't even have the privilege of dying.

By the age of 19, I was a midwifery student at the university. This was also the year of the horrible bombing at the prayer group meeting. I watched the meeting from my television set and was shocked when the explosion went off. Khameneyee was the leading of the group, and while he was injured, unfortunately he was not killed. He lost one hand while other attendees were blown to pieces. After 20 hours, the cleaning crew was still collecting body parts at the university football field. They were disposing them in black plastic trash bags. Brunt pieces of fabric littered the ground and hung from the trees. I went to university the very next day of bombing, I remember walking by the water fountain and seeing a piece of human flesh on the ground. I called the cleaning crew over to collect it.

At that time, I didn't feel anything. I was numb, possibly because the human remains belonged to the enemy. Looking back, I am horrified. When I tell this story to people their faces fill with disgust. I wonder why my reaction to this memory is so detached and dissociated. Sometimes we confuse dissociation with strengths."

I continued processing the memories related to bombing by using art materials using right hand. Image 19 is created, this painting illustrates the bombing in "Namaze Jomeh", Islamic ritual for praying on Fridays. My shoulders are heavy with tension and I feel numb. The numbness is spreading to my hands and makes writing this difficult. I feel frozen, heavy, and sad. Why do people kill for politics, religion, money and power?

I am standing on my feet, aware. I carried this trauma with me for over 30 years. I never spoke of these experiences to anyone. I feel so afraid and numb in this moment; my hands pain me. I feel hopeless, detached, and totally numb.

"Image 19, Bombing"

Now I switched hands and am using my left hand to create a new piece, image 20. My arms are so tired I am having a difficult time painting. None of the colors appeal to me. The empty spaces in the painting scare me, I want to fill them up with color, but I can't seem to choose the right one.

I see a bird; its beak is missing, and it has very ugly wings. Its tail seems to be dragging, stuck in its place. This bird is blind, constipated, and trapped in darkness. When I ask the bird what she sees, she replies: "nothing".

"Image 20, Bombing"

I am using right hand to paint image 21. This painting represents the bombing in the city of Tehran. I remember listening to the news and covering my ears. My eyes are close in horror; I don't want to hear or see this, I can't take it. My sister was on a bus that the bomb went off in the city near her bus, she and her daughter had slight injuries but lots of other people got killed and explode to the pieces. My stomach is in knots as I take it all in. My God! Stop the killing! Stop the pain and suffering! Stop the horror! Stop it!

"Image 21, Bombing"

The heaviness that numbed my hands is dissipating. Now, I have a voice in my head, calling on me to make the killing stop through creative process. I used left hand to create image 22, I see a pregnant girl in this painting. She is trapped and feels disgusted. Her guts twist with a strong vertebra and a strange, pointed creature is attached to the back of her head. I feel like I must liberate her from this creature.

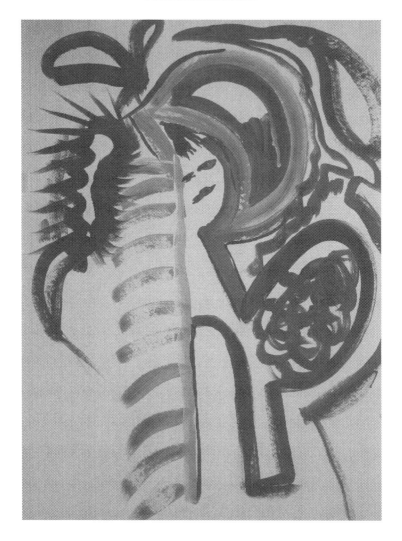

"Image 22, Bombing"

By using right hand to create image 23, I am going through a narrative of visual expressions, non verbal with a deep and more profound meanings, It is like giving a voice to an internal unspoken struggle. In image 23, there is a girl who is a representation of me, and I drew her intentionally to relieve myself of the animal symbolically attached to my head. I only used purple paint for this creation.

I appear to be floating unsteadily. I have no hands or access to help of any kind. The lotus in this painting is ugly and represents a loss of faith and courage in spirit. I feel like I am barely hanging on to my rope and creating art doesn't seem to be helping this time. I am in fight or flight mode, and I feel like I need help. I'm not experiencing any bodily sensations, I'm only aware of my cognitive processing, of being desperate.

I help myself by letting go into the feelings and thoughts that have arisen. I accept them for what they are and will allow them to move without trying to control them. I accept them as the truth, as a part of me. My mind tells me to get out of this state, but I know I am right in the middle of a process, so I continue.

"Image 23, Bombing"

After working on image 24, with my left hand I felt that I am done with this process. I am no longer experiencing any bodily sensations. The heaviness I felt in my hands and tummy is gone.

"Image 24, Bombing"

There is a lot of yellow and white in this painting. I feel a small pain in my back as I observe it. Where is it coming from? The brush strokes are shapeless, a bit stuck. They move softly and slowly. The colors are muddy. I see free particles, and vertebrae. A line separates the muddiness of color and the free particles from each other. The particles may be the only negative representation in this painting. They are trying to attach to my back bones. A splash of color liberates my vertebrae. I am free. My painting tells me I will survive.

Fifth night

The following journal entry illustrates the trauma experienced during a chemical bombing in Iran and other scattered memories.

"At a certain point during the war, our university mandated students to take care of soldiers wounded in chemical bombings. As a midwifery student, I had to work two nights a week. Some of the soldiers were as young as 15years old. The radiation that poisoned their bodies burned my eyes and nose. We wore goggles, masks, gloves, and covers to protect ourselves from radiation. Some of the rooms were so toxic, midwifery students weren't allowed in. I witnessed these young soldiers suffering. They were always hot and thirsty, asking for ice water, and roaming the corridors aimlessly. Some of them were confined to their beds, unable to move.

There was so little I could do for them, I felt useless. All I could think about was getting out of there. I felt sorry for the soldiers as I watched them deteriorate. I remember being overcome with helplessness and hopelessness. My only solution was to escape."

The trace of thoughts jumps from one dark memory to another, I also remembered when I was captured by Islamic law enforcement for no reason without doing anything unlawful or wrong. The new Islamic government harassed people constantly, both in public and privately, in our homes. I was once captured by a Basiji (a member of the police force with the authority to act as a military agent). He didn't have a reason to capture me, but held me captive in the hot, summer heat anyway. He refused to communicate or let me go. I was covered in the uniform assigned to women; a long black jacket that reached my ankles, a long black scarf, pants, socks and shoes. He kept me prisoner in a combat tent for over three hours. I stood the entire time. I begged him to call the police or take me to the station, hoping that someone would help me there. He said nothing, I was his prey and no one else could interfere.

Finally, I begged another Basiji to call the police, and at least take me to prison and to be prosecuted. He phoned a patrol officer who picked me up and took me with the other detained people to a small office. The office served as a prison, and was similar to a holding cell. It was situated in a very dangerous neighborhood. I was terrified. I didn't know where I was, where I was going, or what would happen to me. Upon our arrival, I was so stressed and exhausted, I accidentally slammed my finger in the car door. The pain was excruciating. Shortly after, I was lead into a room and questioned by an officer. He asked me what I had done, and when I told him I had done nothing, he let me go.

They left me in the middle of nowhere, in an unfamiliar and dangerous neighborhood. I walked for two hours to find a bus station, and finally found my way home.

This was one of the most terrifying experiences of my life. Many women in my community were also captured, but they weren't as lucky. Some of them were raped and beaten. I could have ended up like them, and no one would have ever known what happened to me or where to find me."

By recalling all of these horrific memories, I could vividly remember and feel the fear and emotional turmoil in my body, I was ready to pain, I used my right hand to express my feelings visually.

"Image 25"

This painting illustrates my work with the wounded soldiers in the hospital on left side of the image and on right side me inside the tent of the Basiji who captured me. Every image in this painting is gray, like my memories at this time. I can smell the chemicals as I recall the imagery.

I am standing to the side of this painting; ghost like and at a distance, as though I am ready to step off the canvas. I want to escape.

The Islamic government abused the soldiers in this painting. They were betrayed by their own faith and felt they were victims of the war and the poverty of our corrupted society. They believed they were responsible for saving the country and felt entitled to rule people. Many of them blamed the upper class, and projected much of their anger onto the wealthy, especially children of the wealthy. They believed the children were responsible for their misery, and sometimes captured, tortured, and killed them. The government gave these soldiers authority over civilians, making it even harder to survive under this fanatic oppressive government.

On the other side of this painting is a woman in a tent. She is a representation of me upon being captured. I was worried and extremely scared during this experience. The reality of the situation was horrifying; I could be tortured, raped and murdered since it was often happening under these circumstances. I knew I was innocent, but I also knew that didn't matter. I prayed to God to save me. I was scared and helpless. I couldn't run away, these men had guns and wouldn't hesitate to shoot. The consequences would have been severe.

In the painting, I see a whip, gravestones and my screaming face. I ask the man to let me contact a relative or friend, but he refuses.

My feelings upon looking at this painting: It's a scary piece. I feel like I am dead. Somatically, I have no sensations in my body. I can't believe I survived this experience. I am so frightened at this moment; I don't have the capacity to be courageous enough to feel angry. Fear is the only feeling I am present to, fear and sadness.

I use my left hand to create image 26. In this image I see a clean, purple circle dominates the right side of this painting. Other shapes surround it and remind me of closed cases. I think they may represent the traumatic experiences I survived during the revolution and war. They represent my memories involving the religious and political chaos. The purple circle is a representation of me, and the others are significant experiences. All of them are closed. The traumatic memories involving the revolution exist, but they are memories that can rest in the past, no longer having such a negative impact on my present experiences.

A few shapes are outside of the circle that represents my life and experiences, which may indicate that I have not come to terms with all of these memories. Something still needs to be resolved, so I am going to paint this circle again using my right hand.

"Image 26"

Image 27 is created by use of my right hand, at this point I don't feel any fear whatsoever. In this painting, I see a bird. It is nailed to a stick so it stands upright but it cannot fly. Something or someone has clipped its' wings, and now it lives as a powerless and awkward being. The bird is talking to me, she is saying, "can you free me?" "Why do you want to be free?" I asked. The bird states "are you blind, I look deformed and I am not a bird any more I don't look like one." "How can I help you?" I asked. "Unclip this heavy body". I asked, "How can I do that?" The bird replies, "With furthering your drawing".

"Image 27"

As I continue the creative process by use of my left hand, I felt as though I was creating something that represented both victim and survivor. Both are sufferers of trauma. I began using blue to paint a modern bird; it reminds me of one of Picasso's disintegrated pieces.

I see flowers and the tail of the bird in the painting. She (the bird) is free and posing for the picture. The bird feels alive, with scars on her tummy, heart and back. The scars add to her character, and I view them as positive accents. This bird is noble and proud and aware.

"Image 28"

Sixth Night: Green wave; where is my vote?

It took me a bit of time to decide whether or not to include my reaction to the Green Wave Riot in Iran, my dilemma was that the exposure to traumatic experiences in year 2009 doesn't belong to the past and is still current and ongoing, but in the other hand this exposure was a trigger which activated my PTSD. I realized my process wouldn't be complete without exposing and resolving the trauma I experienced from afar.

I was full of anger as I watched the devastation unfold in Iran. I needed to do something for myself since my PTSD was activated. I also felt a huge responsibility to do something for my people. Friends that have come to know me here, in the United States, were surprised by my patriotism and desire to act.

The minute the riot began in Iran, I was triggered by memories so intense, I felt as though the riot was happening outside my own home. The screams of the people on the television were mine, as was the rage, fear, and desperation that radiated off the screen. I was so overcome with emotion that I went to therapy and cried for hours. I spent so much time observing and investigating the coverage. The exposure to violence pushed an internal button, activating the voice inside of me. I knew it was time to speak. I realized I had been repressing so many of the memories and emotions I experienced as the result of politics and religion cruelties. I never healed from those traumas, even in the midst of the beautiful life I now have.

I've never felt any desire to return to Iran, I never even missed my hometown. Watching Iranian movies and listening to Iranian music depressed me, so I avoided it. I didn't realize the reason for that was because I never processed my old pain. The scars on my psyche were fresh after all these years, and I knew I had to do something about it. I decided to conduct a heuristic research experiment with myself, knowing that I would never regain my fullest mental potential and clarity until I engaged these feelings. I would have to work through a process of re-traumatization to find the core issues behind these feelings. I did this in part for Neda, Sohrab and all the others whose names I don't know, but whose beauty I remember, those who got murdered and tortured and raped for freedom."

I started painting with right hand and creating image 29, while painting the only thoughts would ring in my head was, "where is my vote?"

A green ocean covers the canvas of this painting, the green waves churn to claim freedom and power for humanity. Dark forces threaten this ocean of freedom and pollute its peaceful waters with the bodies of those murdered, raped, tortured, and dismembered. All of this happened under the guise of so called "God". Kidnapped women were burned to death after being raped; this ocean has become an open burial for them. One of the dark forces urinates on the God that politic has created for him, he does this to free his soul.

"Image 29"

I witnessed these atrocities with my own eyes. I feel so, extremely sad. I feel heavy and my eyes burn looking at this piece. I am unable to cry. I remember that last summer after I was viewing these crimes on youtube clips I became so overwhelmed that I broke one of my toes on accident. I feel so sad, I could cry enough tears to fill this ocean, but I don't seem to have any tears left.

Image 30 is created by use of left hand as a respond to all these dark memories, this painting is black, dark and chaotic. I feel disgusted, disturbed and annoyed just looking at it. I see two killer whales; one of them is being skinned. There is a dismembered hand at the bottom of the stormy ocean. The whales are unhappy, they long to jump from the dark water and escape to another place. The black whale asks the other, "Are you in pain?"

"A little," he responds. "But if I maneuver my body and go straight, I may be able to escape."

"No, it won't work after all," he says. "But maybe you can, maybe you can go, be free and be healed." I feel scared looking at this painting and engaging in this dialogue. I feel odd sensations throughout my body, especially in my head.

"Image 30"

I pursue the process by using right hand, to paint the image 31. I think by now I have enough trust in the creative process and I am eagerly hoping to release the emotional pains and externalize them on the paper.

Scribble, I don't know what to paint. To illustrate the plight of humanity, the wars, destruction and chaos, seems impossible. There's too much going on and none of it makes any sense. My darkest nightmares are becoming reality. This prison holds all of our power, freedom and blood captive. It seems ridiculous and unreal that something like this could occur.

"Image 31"

At this point my rational mind is taking a seat of observer and has no desire to make sense of what is revealing in front of it. I continue painting with left hand and creating image 32.

A battle unfolds in this painting. The circular shapes represent the spirits of victims soaring through the sky. They seem to be in fight with dark forces and suffering with extreme pain. A weapon- like entity is being under attack of the souls, but its power is unstable. They are accessible from the side and something is coming to get them.

Wars are brutal and only complete with atrocious experiences. I was prisoner to those experiences for a long time. Now, my feelings of sadness have been transformed into courage and I am going to fight; to be a warrior of light. There is a battle between light and dark, and I believe the light will triumph

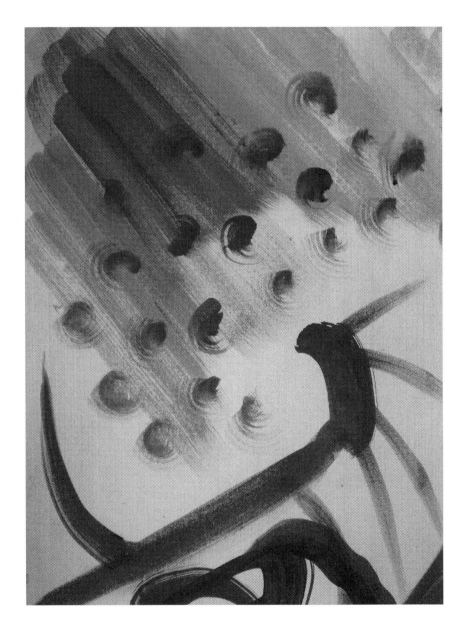

"Image 32"

PART 11
Data Analysis and Symbolic Meanings

Analysis of Data

The first step in the analysis process was to review each of the seven sessions of paintings individually, and also reading the journal entries for each session. As themes emerged from each of these individual sessions they began to cluster across the sessions. These clusters then became the focus of the results of the analysis. The themes emerged during the illumination phase include use of color, the use of lines and intensity of brush strokes, organization, containment, shapes, metaphors in imagery, representations of self, representations of familial influences.

Colors:

Although there was a full spectrum of colors available, the same colors were used unintentionally in each painting that I created throughout the immersion process. This was a revelation that emerged in the analysis process; the primary colors used were red, black, dark purple and dark brown. These colors portrayed violence, fear and suffering. Fear and aggression were communicated with dark colors. The dark purple became lighter throughout the course of the process and mostly present in work created using the left hand. The paintings produced with the left hand gradually evolved with the use of yellows and oranges, two of my favorite colors that always bring warmth to my heart.

Lines and Shapes and their correlation with body sensations and emotions:

During the illumination process the lines and shapes began to emerge as a theme which was correlated to the colors and emotions. Each series started with lines that appear chaotic and disorganized in the initial paintings. Strong brush strokes also covered the canvases. During each session strong emotions were expressed while lines and brush strokes were strong and sharp, the colors also were dark with red in them. I also noticed use of art media and darker color helped me to release painful emotions. The chaotic and disorganized nature of the earliest artworks, created using the right hand, helped me to relieve the emotions associated with my most painful memories at the time of creation. During the illumination process, I realized the paintings with pointy and broken lines were drawn while experiencing feelings of anger and rage. Thick and curvy lines represented emotions associated with tremendous fear.

Animals:

Cats and Lions: In early nights of the process I noticed cat and female lions in most of the art pieces. In each painting, the lions were either a target of violence or trapped. The lions stood tall and strong, grand and waiting, but disappointment was present in her gaze. Gradually, the lion began to disappear and was slowly replaced with trapped birds. Birds became one of the most dominant subjects of imagery presented in most of the paintings. The birds presented themselves as being either stuck in place or nailed to a strong vertical line. They were always either injured or deformed and strongly desired the ability to fly. One of the other imagery was Wales who were two and one was injured.

Representation of self:

During the illumination phase I have realized that I have represented myself in many different forms and shapes and animals. The images of girls without feet and hands were prevalent in most of the paintings. If the body was complete, it appeared robotic and frozen. The presence of the girl without hands allowed me to acknowledge my helplessness as a woman while living in Islamic country.

In many of the pieces, the girl is covering her eyes or her face. She sometimes has her hands over her ears to deafen the noise of disruption and chaos. The images communicate how horrific the crimes committed during the revolution really were.

Body Sensation:

Throughout the entire immersion process I experienced intense bodily sensations which were recorded in journals at each session. In response to the process of art making in each session I experienced either pain in my jaw or shoulders, stomach and or back. In each session by progressing the art making and releasing negative emotions my body began to feel lighter. The desire to end producing art in each session was in harmony with calmness, fading the unpleasant body sensations and disappearing negative emotions.

Family

This process was a very solitary exploration. At no point was my family present in any of the artwork I created. I was always alone, both in the journal entries and paintings. This was despite my family's strong presence and the shared traumatic experiences we were exposed to during revolution. I could not have survived without their love and support. This process represented the journey within me. It was a process that helped me regain my own individuation. The findings might suggest that, because I was an adolescent during the revolution, I wasn't secure enough to develop my own identity. It was crucial that this immersion process was a solitary activity and the arts address that clearly.

Duality:

Manifestations of duality held a strong presence throughout the entirety of the artworks. This was especially obvious with pieces of work created using the left hand and in the mid process of art making. Representations of duality usually emerged in images of birds, whales, or when the art was displayed in two sections. In each presentation, the duality was used to communicate either strength and power or extreme suffering and death. The dialogue among the dual representations always communicated ideas to encourage either feelings related to strength or helplessness. When I felt strong I knew that if I continued to serve my process I would find freedom. When I was weak, all I wanted to do was escape.

I also experienced that I was searching for answer to cruelty on humans resulted from politic and or religion. After indwelling into my inner world and life experiences I realized my search is like running after mirage with a hope to get to water. Through conducting this heuristic process, I realized that I have no answer to why the cruelty is happening, but I have gained clarity to what has happened to me. I have explored some of my coping strategies that I employed at the time of exposure to traumatic experiences 30 years ago. I also have gained wisdom of accepting the traumatic experiences without hatred and resentment as part of my life reality and acknowledge their painful effects and the suffering in the past and liberate myself from them. I have gained a stage of acceptance and acknowledgment about yes crulty exists and yes politics and religion are the great tool for target humanity through their belief and yes we all are controlled by imposed fear through them. My role is to see myself clearly and not to identify with the perpetrator or victim.

Coping mechanisms and survival strategies visible in the art.

I realized my employed coping strategy was suppressing the traumatic memories to unconscious by referring to the images of girls covering eyes, ears, or face, I didn't want to see or hear or even understand what was happening to the surrounding around me or to me, these arts were produced with right hand which as suggested by Talwar is related to the left brain the analytic mind which shows I deliberately was trying to suppress the material. The exposure to traumatic event made me freeze. I was in the state of shock which made me frozen in the images and took me to the state of no hands or feet, representing helplessness and hopelessness. Also in the imagery the repression of the traumatic experiences was evidence since by delving into the traumatic memories I released strong emotions such as anger and rage and extreme sadness, and the unpleasant body sensations. These strong expressions of emotions were evidence of the catharsis effect.

Use of the ATTP method made visible the symptoms of complex trauma;

Use of the journaling at start of the process helped me to stimulate memories and organized my thoughts around a specific traumatic experience, and then the urge of creating art emerged unwittingly. Talwar's ATTP protocol made the process of self-expression natural. The flow of art making, and the release of emotions seemed very easy with no difficulty or resistance. I felt open and connected to the process. As I mentioned before I had the problem of accessing my traumatic experiences in verbal therapy but no difficulty to revisit the trauma through this process.

Through the employed art therapy method I realized that I used to experience difficulty and impairment in both of these areas, identifying the accurate effect of the traumatic experiences on me and expressing the accurate emotions at the time by use of the defense mechanisms such as suppression, repressions, and dissociation which were evident in the arts. Because of these difficulties I displayed symptoms of dissociation, the chronic numbing of emotional experience. I was also developed dysphoria, maladaptive coping strategies, and began avoiding of all emotional experiences related to Iran, including positive experiences.

The left-hand process which is related to right brain helped me to observe the unconscious effects of witnessing those violence and traumas on my psyche and observe myself as a prisoner. In the produced arts I observed how myself representation changed from lion to duality of injured birds and Wales. I saw my splitting of self in the imagery and was able through the process of art making and catharsis to put the split selves back together and make a whole person. The apparent symptoms in the arts were, dissociation, repression and suppressing materials.

The use of the ATTP resolve symptoms related to complex trauma;

Through Talwar method I was able to re- experience my Physical sensations and release of emotions which I did not released at the time of exposure to past traumatic experiences. I also was able to identify the physical sensations which were outside conscious awareness and their repetitive presence. Talwar method helped me to identify the emotional state, bodily sensations and their relationship with the images of traumatic events and helped me to accurately express my emotions and calm my internal mental state.

By identifying the employed defense mechanism at the time of the exposure to trauma from age 14-27, I was able to let go of them and allow myself to form a healthier self-concept as a woman.

Meanings

After conducting the immersion and illumination phases, as well as the emerged themes, I began studying literature related to political and religious violence and the psychological effects it imposes on humans, especially on children and adolescents. I was amazed at how similar those findings were to the conclusions I drew from my explication process. It turns out that the experience I had were, in fact universal; from the victims of genocide in Africa to the observers of war in Cambodia, the psychological scars inflicted by human cruelty are the same.

I found that my childhood traumatic experiences led to the multiple symptoms found in complex trauma and as a result it created chaos in my life and changed my schema about the world and myself. Grossman (2003) suggests that the ongoing, persistent and continuous violence, may form an integral part of each individual's internal world, identity, values, beliefs and history. The traumatic experiences effect a part of their present, and also inform who each person will become.

During my immersion process, feelings of humiliation associated with trauma and the capacity to protect myself and others reappeared. I felt betrayed and extremely angry by the nature of the violence perpetuated by religion and politics. My art exposed clear feelings of helplessness at this point. My world view was drastically affected by the exposure to war trauma; I was uncertain about the reliability and predictability of the world, I had problems with boundaries and became distrustful and suspicious of others.

This mental state used to hold me hostage in a state of fear and anxiety. The anticipation and anxiety became part of my identity, and it instilled a sense of insecurity and being over involved and overwhelmed with maintaining safety. Donnelly et al. suggest that when a person is severely traumatized, it is normal that they cannot integrate the extent of the experience they have undergone all at once. The traumatized individual's view of the world is severely changed.

Cook et al. also explain that dissociation is one of the key responses in victims of complex trauma and limits the capability of integrating emotions and experiences. It is a defense mechanism used to protect the mind by disconnecting thoughts and emotions. This defense is also known as the freeze response. Through the undertaken research and conducting the Art Therapy Trauma Protocol I was able to explore the horrific experiences and recognize and address the dissociation. Through the release of intense emotions during the process of art making and analysis of the data, I realized that I developed the dissociation as a protection against the exposure. I realized my mind was protected by employing this defense mechanism from full impact of the trauma which that could also be related to my vulnerable age at the time. One of the themes in the analysis section of the arts was barriers, it seemed that unconsciously I was trying to block the environmental crisis by covering my face or ears or eyes. I witnessed moments so traumatizing I dissociated or tried to deny that they ever happened.

I remember during the war and the time of bombardment in Iran, making art was my rescue. One afternoon I was putting varnish on one of my paintings, due to premature application, the paint started peeling off. At that time the Iraqi airplanes started bombarding the city and civilians. I didn't pay attention to the sound of explosions or shudder of my room's windows or floor despite my parents yelling at me to take cover to a safe place. Instead I ignored the danger and focused even more on what I was doing and kept cleaning the varnish off my painting. Through this research process I realized that I was dissociated from the sense of danger, I could only feel the danger of destroying my painting not the danger of losing my life.

DSM IV explains that the traumatized person will experience feelings similar to extreme fear, helplessness and horror during and post the initial traumatic experience. The memories and emotions associated with the distressing event can continue affecting a person's life for years. During my art exploration I clearly saw the signs of being traumatized and feeling of helplessness, fear, rage and anger. In the self-representations, there were images with missing feet and hands which indicated my sense of helplessness. The images of wounded and trapped birds and animals lead me to conclude that I was entrapped by my traumatic experiences. Each injury and scar represent a traumatic memory I witnessed and lived through, and left me in the state of stagnation, helpless and hopelessness.

Then I realized that even after the cessation of traumatizing experiences until recent I was living in state of alert and vigilance. I was consumed with horrific mental images of all the terrible things that could happen to me and my loved ones. These intrusive images would burst into my mind not as the typical flashbacks but related to current situations and my family. I would then visualize how I would escape and save my loved ones in those situations. As I grew older, I learned to numb myself to the negative images that I couldn't stop. I learned to accept what I thought at the time was a normal part of my brain function and gradually gave them less and less validation.

I realized that these mental images are like flash backs or the signs of PTSD. After conducting this research, I realized that each horrific image was draining me from vital energy that could be channeled into sincerely enjoying life. I realized that every insignificant sign of caution would trigger negative imagery and I would automatically take mental action to protect myself. After revisiting my traumatic experiences by use of the Art Therapy Trauma Protocol and releasing associated emotions and integrating them, the negative mental imagery began to fade in its consistency and is replaced with more empowering thoughts and images that frees me from the suffering and distrust I struggled with for so many years.

There are four characteristics related to childhood trauma. The four characteristics are as follow: 1) repetitive behaviors, 2) trauma-specific fears, 3) changed attitudes about people, life, and the future, 4) visualized or repeatedly perceived memories of the traumatic event. Throughout conducting this research, I gained awareness that my negative mental images were related to the trauma that I experienced during religious revolution and war.

The traumatized individual's mind is frequently unable to allow the full impact of the event into consciousness. The traumatic memory exists in a highly charged sensory state that trigger in flashbacks, nightmares, and arousal states that occur with reminders of the original event. By using Art Therapy Trauma Protocol, I was able to allow the full impact of the traumatic experiences into my consciousness and release the charged sensory.

In affirmation to my experience I found that one of the aspects of trauma is the feeling of humiliation in regard with the person's capacity to protect themselves or others. Trauma experiences may include feelings of severe loss, anger, betrayal, and helplessness. Loss can be manifested in loss of a sense of safety and security. I realized anger, helplessness and rage were dominant in my expressive arts and I have released lots of emotions attached to loss of sense of safety and security. During immersion process I re-experienced the feeling of humiliation connected with my capacity to protect myself and others and I felt sever anger, betrayal by the violence perpetrated by religion and politics. In my arts I could clearly see myself as a helpless individual. I realized the exposure to trauma caused me to conclude that the world is not and may never be the same because of what happened. I processed all feelings associated with this thought process with my therapist. At my therapy sessions I was able to look at the arts and discuss the feelings and emotions associated to with my therapist. Feeling of anger and rage has manifested in my produced art by use of black and red color, as Betensky (1995) explains that the use of color black is common for individuals who cope with sickness, trauma, or loss.

Now I feel all those released emotions and feelings at the time of immersion are evolving into an understanding and balance of identity. As Levin (1982) describes seven developmental stages in human development needs to be met to form an identity. The stage from age 13-19 is the recycling stage which is called Integration. The seventh stage—formally named Recycling—covers all our adult years. Levin suggests that over the course of adulthood, we return to the themes and issues of the earlier stages with new opportunities to "grow through" the developmental issues each stage represents. We either encounter or can create opportunities to revisit each stage as many times as we need to.

After revisiting my traumatic experiences by use of ATTP I realized my sense of self as an adolescent was damaged, Figure 13 illustrates a faceless young and vibrant adolescent in the middle of horrific danger. I felt this image represented me at age 14, searching for my identity. After the extremist's Islamic government mandated women to cover their hair and deprived us from our social rights then I saw how I transformed into a frozen monster, helpless, depressed and hopeless (Figure 16).

I realized that as an adolescent, I identified with living in the midst of danger, but I never felt alone. I always had my family and friends with me. Adolescents' responses to the adversities of war is safe guarded by both parents and educators although they respond more to the world beyond their families' reactions to the experience of war. Bandura (1973) and Rotter (1942) further that the effect of the environment and interaction of the adolescent with the environment will make their personality. The personality is internal and also responsive to the external environmental stimuli. Personality is a relatively stable set of potentials for responding to situations in a particular way. In my creative process I realized that in early adolescence my identity transformed from a strong lion to the suffering, wounded birds. The duality here is discussed more fully below.

Trauma in childhood categorizes into two type, type I trauma includes "full, detailed memories, "omens" and misperceptions. Type II trauma includes denial and numbing, self hypnosis and dissociation, and rage. In my artwork I could see clearly the expression of anger through strong brush strokes and use of black and red color. Most notably I drew tears as blood which displays strong expression of anger and sadness at the same time. I realized that I also represented myself numb and frozen with an emotionless face. Trauma begins with the events outside the child. Once the events take place, a number of internal changes occur in the child which lasts. The changes stay active for years-often to the detriment of the young victim. I was carrying all the internal changes with me as unresolved psychological reactions which manifested themselves as negative response to Iran and being Iranian and my mistrust of world affairs. I denied my country of origin and cultural identity so that I could distance myself from the history that was buried in my psyche.

As Kaplan reported in his study with survivors of the Holocaust, they have displayed self-image as well as a displayed fragmented self because of the massive trauma they witnessed. The fragmented self in survivors became evident while they were interviewed about their experiences; most of them used "I" without noticing they were not actually speaking about themselves. Before I completed this research I shared the same fragmented self that the author describes, I could talk about the massive trauma without displaying any emotions. I wasn't conscious of the destructive effects of witnessing the horrible violence. Through the art therapy process I released so many aches in my body and painful emotions and tears. By crying through creation of the women's right artwork, I realized that developing a gender identity in Islamic country was a huge challenge and burden on me during my early adolescence.

Kalmanowitz and Lloyd caution that witnessing a violent act even if we do not experiencing it directly promotes rigid and compulsive thinking. They assert that witnessing the act of violence can also be through watching the media such as television. Viewing the media can provoke emotional reactions and perpetuate polarities in thinking. The witness either identifies with the victim or the aggressor in order to end the psychological pressure. The longer the political violence lasts, the alienation and dehumanization increases in social levels The authors explain that people exposed to political violence do act impulsively which can shock them. The unpredictability of how the witness will respond can result in "hot" tempers that keep the victim in numbness, cutoff, detached and even apathetic. In mass destruction survivors don't display emotional pain or mourning, but instead it is replaced with numb sensation or anesthesia. He suggests that in this state, it is also impossible to cope with the guilt of surviving.

As the result of my position as a witness to cruelty to humans I experienced dehumanization when I witnessed horror and violence directed to my perceived enemies. In Figure 19 this dehumanization is represented, I was numb and frozen and felt many somatic responses in my body. I respond to Figure (20), I wrote in my journal that I am a bird again, with no beaks (nothing has to say, no voice), ugly and heavy wings and stuffed and heavy tail that is keeping the bird grounded. I was trapped and helpless and disabled.

Some of the global negative effect of war trauma on adolescents are high level of anxiety, somatic complains and PTSD. Most notably the author identifies a hindering of interpersonal trust, curtailing the threshold for stress endurance. By referring to the theme of lines and brush strokes, the disorganized and chaotic shapes in the arts suggest the level of anxiety.

The individuals who have had a normal and nurturing upbringing do achieve self-worth and compassionate and positive assumption about the world. She also noted that exposure to horrifying and terrifying cruelty on humans do challenge those assumptions and destroy them, the damage is hard to rebuild. To confirm Janof-Bulma's claim I had a normal and nurturing upbringing with no experience of any significant trauma, and I did achieve self-worth and positive assumptions about the world. After the exposure to cruelty and crime on humanity through Islamic religious revolution and war at age 14, my assumption was shattered and my search for identity became stagnated in time and trapped in anxiety and fear. I assert that rebuilding positive assumption about the world and self-worth was possible for me through ATTP in the undertaken research.

In Jung's view "the psyche is made of opposites; that is, any conscious attitude has its opposite in an unconscious one. These opposites manifest themselves in culture as well as in the psychological development of the individual. The collective unconscious is a layer in the psyche, which underlies the personal unconscious" . The collective unconscious is the least accessible of the psyche material. The collective unconscious is expressed through archetypes, which are instinctual patterns which have no forms in their own right; they are not tangible, nor visible, but rather sense perceptions. They may constellate in dreams, myth and art.

During the analysis of data, I recognized dualities in my artwork that were illustrated by animals, symbols and shapes. I realized the duality came to play in my arts while I used my non dominant (left hand), responsible for activating of right brain which refers to intuitive mind or my unconscious. I have found that these two manifested opposites such as two whales in one art or the two birds in the other art. During the illumination process these two symbols had a dialog, which was then recorded in a journal entry. As reference to Jung in the above passage my psyche clearly demonstrated the simultaneous duality of 'victim' and 'survivor' through different shapes and patterns as sense perception that only manifested through my interpretations of the artwork. The duality in archetypes presented in my art led me to conclude that the archetypes are in tension of opposites in my own unconscious. The overwhelming traumatic experiences that I was exposed to in my vulnerable adolescent development created an archetypal split that was not integrated until I was able to process the events utilizing the ATTP.

Edward (2001) explains that "Archetypal factors are inescapable but determined behavior negatively only when they remain completely unconscious. By allowing a sense of participation and dialogue with archetypal (and personal) material in personified form, the patient can integrate unacknowledged aspects of personality and, with increased consciousness, come to better terms with life. This might be described as the ability to live within one's personal myth rather than be lived by it" (Edward in Rubin, 2001. P87). I entered into a relationship with my symbolic archetypal images; I became aware of a disintegrated self. The process of the ATTP and analysis of data brought awareness and a sense of wholeness restored a sense of balance. I felt relief from intense psychological and physical and emotional symptoms. By utilizing ATTP I was able to detect and externalize the duality in my archetypes 'victim' and 'survivor'. I was able to observe their struggle and to allow the images to provide a context to contemplate the fear and perceived ideas of the experienced trauma and allow the images to speak what they needed to say to come to balance.

Base on my findings by undertaking this research, I propose that in this case the victim, survivor archetypes created a split, under different life circumstances one of the two plays a psychological role in a specific context or time and the other one remains hidden in the shadow. My supposition is that when these dualities come to balance is the individual reaches clarity and peace of mind. However, when a person is exposed to a traumatic experience the instilled fear causes the dual archetypes to emerge as a split, which causes confusion and anxiety and other psychological problems.

I was aware that this emergent process would force me to delve deeper into my awareness, by knowing the trauma elements and its effect on my identity. One of the reasons I suffered so much was my attachment to the memories of trauma, the images of the scared birds, and the skinned whale represented my deep attachment to the trauma. I had to accept and acknowledge the victim part of me to integrate this part of my history so that I could be whole. As the result, the part of me that is true and strong, my subconscious and soul, was able to push through the process, engaging the trauma and then emerging into freedom. At this point, the symbols representing duality came into balance, in more complete terms, the traumatized parts of me lost its negative influence in order to manifest strength and re-emerge with my psyche intact. This relieved my pain and suffering. My partitioned traumatic memories were like chains, keeping me prisoner and preventing me from living a joyful life. I will never forget them, but now they don't plague me as flashbacks and images to be repressed and ignored but simply a part of my history that can be recalled at will.

The process of becoming a well-balanced, whole individual never would have flourished if I had continued to maintain the fragmented identity I developed because of my traumatic experiences. I was two people; on one side, I was a victim, scared, broken, and suffering. On the other, I was a survivor, strong and resilient. I had to come face to face with both sides of my identity, and look at myself, not as victim or survivor, but as an individual who has experienced both pain and joy.

Creative Synthesis

You, the reader, now are the witness, the witness to cruelty on humanity through my inner journey. You witnessed cuts of knife of political and religious violence on my psyche. You witnessed me, "the witness" you looked at a witness's mindscape.

After conducting this research, I am a happier person, and culturally, I realized that I have no shame or guilt, or anger attached to be an Iranian. I noticed I like to view news from Iran without being overwhelmed by rage or sadness. I noticed that I have stronger acquaintance with ancient Persia and enjoy my favorite poems. I felt a secure connection to my original ancestry of glamorous Iran. I feel proud and honored to be an Iranian and having the blood of the originator of humanity and human rights in my veins. Iran, to me, is glamorous, sacred, and beautiful because it is carrying spiritual values, not only a history of pain and suffering. I realized Iran is invaded and raped by religion for centuries. We Iranians who are victims of the oppressive Islamic regime of Iran need healing on national and personal levels. Both are important, and one without the other is superficial and shallow. While it was necessary to reach the point to express my despair and renewal, I began to understand what healing from the past trauma entailed. It is humbling to realize that those still living in Iran face a far more significant challenge. The complex traumatic processing has come to an end and has been immensely helpful. I have gained clarity. I don't view myself from the scope of my weakest moments. I accept that the world is sometimes full of negativity and brutality, but I also realize we are agents for change. We are all-powerful and capable of surviving. I am here to help to manifest healing for humanity through my work as an art therapist. We all are light soldiers. I used to be in limbo, stuck in-between light and dark thoughts, but not anymore. I am in the battle now, proudly serving the light in the world of darkness.

The art that I created for creative synthesis is called "Metamorphosis." It is familiar it is personal, it is not stagnated, I can see movement and growth, I can see the emergence and harmony (Figure 33). The process of indwelling into my memories of past traumas was dramatic and extremely emotional. It transformed my life and permitted a spiritual metamorphosis from being trapped and broken to sublime. My transformation was clarity of understanding, a willingness to open up and learn, and the conscious effort to see the small miracles and mysteries unfolding through this process.

The most important milestones for me were to learn to accept instead of rejecting out of fear. The image 33, illustrates an ocean of life which is moving. Through the creative process, the duality emerged; the movements in the yellow sky on the right side are showing a cocoon. The cocoon refers to the memories of trauma and pain that I went through. In the sky on the left side, the bright colors of light and life were trying to help me to survive. When these two different aspects came to harmony and balanced the freedom emerged. The metamorphosis happened, and the butterfly became free from the cocoon of pain and suffering, and the survivor side of the painting bloomed to life and beauty, which is represented by flowers. I love my life with all its memories and honor it for the lessons it entailed. Sometimes, I had to give up things that I cherished the most and experience pain and suffering. But, in that sacrifice was always a valuable lesson and gift. Metamorphosis of the spirit is a challenging task. But if we allow it to happen… we enter into the cocoon as a caterpillar and emerge as a beautiful butterfly ready to take flight.

"Our task is not to seek for love, but merely to seek and find all the barriers within ourselves that we have built against it".   "Rumi".

"Image 33, Creative synthesis"

REFERENCES

Bandura, A. (1977). Social Learning Theory. New Jersey, NY: Prentice Hall.

Bandura, A. (1973). Aggression: A Social Learning Analysis. Englewood Cliffs, NJ: Prentice- Hall.

Betensky, G. M. (1995). What Do You See: Phenomenology of Therapeutic Art Expression, London: Jessica Kingsley.

Boscarino, J. (2000). Post War experiences of Vietnam veterans. In G. Fink (Ed.), Encyclopedia of stress,(pp. 3,656-661). San Diego, CA: Academic Press.

Bronfman, E., Campis, B., & Koocher, G.P. (1998). Helping children to cope: Clinical issues for acutely injured and medically traumatized children. Professional psychology: Research and Practice. 29: 574-581.

Case, C. (1996). On the Aesthetic Moment in the Transference. Inscape, 1(2), 39-45.

Chemtob, C., Tolin, D., Pitman, R.K., & Van Der Kolk, B.A. (2000). Eye movement desensitization and reprocessing. In E.B. Foa, T. Keane and M. Friedman (Eds.) Treatment guidelines for Post Traumatic Stress Disorder. New York: Guilford Press

Clarkson, P. (1988). Conflict, confusion and deficit. The European Journal for Counseling, psychology and Healt,2(4), 6-13.

Cohen, J.A., Deblinger,E., Mannarin, A. (2004). Trauma focused cognitive behavioral therapy for sexually abused children. Psychiatric Times, 21 (10).

Compas, B.E., Nakarne, V. L., & Fondacavo, K.M. (1988). Coping with stressful events in older children and younger adolescents. Journal of consulting and clinical psychology, 56, 405-411.

Cook, A., Spinazzola, J., Ford, J., Lanktree, C., Blaustein, M. Cloitre, M., DeRosa, R., Hubbard, R., Kagan, R., Liautaud, J., Mallah, K., Olafson, E., & Van der Kolk, B. (2005). Complex trauma in children and adolescents. Psychiatric Annals, 35, 390-398.

Cook, A., Blaustein, M., Spinazzola, J., & Van der Kolk, B. (Eds.). Complex trauma in children and adolescents. National Child Traumatic Stress Network. www.nctsnet.org/nccts/nav

Corr, C.A., Nabe, C.M., & Corr, D.M. (2000). Death and dying, life and living (3rd Ed.). Belmony, CA: Wadsworth.

Complex Trauma in Children and Adolescents, Retrieved from, National Child Traumatic Stress Network [NCTSN], www.NCTSNet.org

Cook, A., Blaustein, M., Spinazzola, J., and Van der Kolk, B., (2005). Complex Trauma in Children and Adolescents.Psychiatric Annals, 35(5), 390-398.

Cox, M., Theilgaard, A. (1997). Mutative Metaphors in Psychotherapy: The Aeolian Mode, London: Jessica Kingsley

Cozolino, L. (2002). The Neuroscience of Psychotherapy Building and Rebuilding the Human brain. New York: W.W.Norton & Company, Inc

Craig, E. (1978). The Heart of the Teacher: A heuristic study of the inner world of teaching. (Doctoral dissertation, Boston University). Dissertation Abstracts International, 38, 7222A. cited at Mustakas, C. E., (1990).

Cymberknopf, S. (1996). The art of repairing: Fifty one years after the Holocausts. Unpublished Master's thesis presented to Goldsmiths College, Art Psychotherapy Unit, University of London. Cited at the book Art therapy refugees, by Dokter.

Desivilya, H.S., Gal, R., & Ayalon, O. (1996). Long-term effects of trauma in adolescence: Comparison between survivors of a terrorist attack and control counterparts. Anxiety, stress, and Coping, 9, 135-150.

Dokter, D. (1998). Arts Therapists, Refugees and Migrants Reaching Across Borders. Jessica Kingsley Publishers. London and Philadelphia.

Donnelly, J., Kovacova, A., Osofsky, J., Osofsky, H., Paskell, C., Salem-Pickartz, J., (2004).

Developing strategies to Deal with Trauma in Children: A means of ensuring conflict prevention, security and social stability. The NATO

Program for Security through Science. Nato Security through Science Series E: Human and Societal Dynamics- Vol. 1

Dorahy, M. J. (1998). Trauma-induced dissociation and psychological effects of the 'trouble' in Northern Ireland: An overview and integration. Irish Journal of Psychology, 19(2-3), 332-344.

Dube, S.R., Anda, R.F., Felitti, V.J., Chapman, D.P., Williamson, D. F., Giles, W.H. (2001). Childhood Abuse, Household Dysfunction, and the Risk of Attempted suicide Throughout the Lifespan: Findings from the adverse childhood experiences study. Journal of the American Medical Association, 286 (24), 3089 American Psychiatric Association. (2000). Diagnostic and statistical manual of mental disorders (Revised 4th ed.). Washington, DC: Author

Erikson, E. H. (1982). The life cycle completed. New York: Norton.

Finkelhor, D. & Kendall-Tackett, K.A. (1997). A developmental perspective on the childhood impact of crime, abuse and violent victimization. In D. Cicchetti & S. Toth (Eds.) Rochester Symposium on Developmental Psychopathology: Developmental Perspectives on Trauma, . 8. (pp. 1-32). Rochester, NY: University of Rochester Press.

Fishman, Y., & Ross, J. (1990). Group treatment for exiled survivors of torture. American Journal of Orthopsychiatry, 60, 135–142.

Fonagy, P. (1998). "Attachment, the Holocaust and the outcome of child psychoanalysis: The Third Generation." Paper presented at the 3rd Congress of the European Federation for Psychoanalytic Psychotherapy on the Public Sector, Cologne, Germany, 28 March.

Foy, D. W., Eriksson, C. B., & Trice, G. A. (2002). Introduction to group interventions for trauma survivors. Group Dynamics: Theory, Research, and Practice, 5, 246–251

Freud, A., & Burlingham, D. (1943). War and children. New York: International University Press.

Gal, R. (1998). Colleageues in distress: "Helping the helpers." International review of psychiatry, 10, 234.

Garbarino, J., & Kostelny, K. (1993). Children's response to war: what do we know? La Greca, A. M., Silverman, W. K., Vernberg, E.M., Roberts, M. C. (2002) Helping children cope with disasters and terrorism. American Psychological Association. 17, 446 .

Golub D. (1984) 'Symbolic expression in post-traumatic stress disorder: Vietnam combat veterans in art therapy', The Arts in Psychotherapy, 12:285-296.

Green, A.H., & Kocijan-Hercigonja, D. (1988). Stress and coping in children traumatized by war. Journal of the American Academy of Psychoanalysis, 26, 585-597.

Grossman, D. (2003). Elective affinities by Ari Shavit' Haaretz newspaper, Haaretz magazine, 10 January. Cited by Kalmanowitz, D. and Lloyd B. (2005), Art therapy and political violence, with art, without illusion, Routlege. PP 21.

Hamblen, J. (1998), äPractice Parameters for the Assessment and Treatment of Children and Adolescents with Posttraumatic Stress Disorder, ä Journal of the American Academy of Child and Adolescent Psychiatry, 37:10 supplement.

Hobfoll, S.E., & Lilly, R. S. (1993). Resource conservation as a strategy for community psychology. Journal of community psychology, 21, 128-148.

Jacobs, S. C. (1999). Traumatic grief: Diagnosis, treatment, and prevention. New York: Brunner/Mazel.

Janoff-bulman, R. (1992). Shattered Assumptions: Towards a New Psychology of Trauma. New York free press.

Johnson, D.R. (1987), The role of the creative arts therapies in the diagnosis and treatment of psychological trauma. The Arts in Psychotherapy, 14: 7-13.

Judd, L. L. (1967). The Normal Psychological Development of the American Adolescent—A Review, California Medicine. 107(6): 465–470.

Jung, C.G. (1989). Memories, Dreams and Reflections. Vintage Book Edition. U.S.

Jung, C.G. (1971). "The Spiritual Problem of Modern Man", Civilization in Transition. Vol 10, The Collected Works of Carl G. Jung, tr. R.F.C. Hull. Bollingen Series XX. Princeton University Press

Jung, C.G. (1959). The Archetypes and the Collective Unconscious. CWP Pt 1. Princeton: Bollingen. Book Dokter.

La Greca, A. M., Silverman, W. K., Vernberg, E.M., Roberts, M. C. (2002) Helping children cope with disasters and terrorism. American Psychological Association. 17, 446.

Laor N., Wolmer L, Cohen D. (2001). Mother's functioning and children's syndrome five years after a scub missile attack. American journal psychiatry. 158, 1020-1026.

Laub, D. (2005). From speechlessness to narrative: The cases of Holocust historians and of psychiatrically hospitalized survivors. Literature and Medicine, 24 (2):253-265.

Laub, D., & Auerhahn, N. C. (1993). Knowing and not knowing massive trauma: Forms of traumatic memory. International Journal of Psychoanalysis, 74, 287-302.

Lazarus, R.S., & Folkman, S. (1984). Stress, appraisal, and coping. New York: Springer.

Levin, P. (1982). The cycle of development. Transactional Analysis Journal, 12, 2, 129-139.

Lieberman, A. F., van Horn, P., Grandison, C. M., & Pekarsky, J. H. (1997). Mental health assessment of infants, toddlers, and preschoolers in a service program and a treatment outcome research program. Infant Mental Health Journal, 18, 158-170.

Lifton, R.J. (1969). Death in life: Survivors of Hiroshima. New York: Random House.

Kaplan Suzanne, (2006). Children in genocide: Extreme traumatizatio and the "affect propeller". International Journal of Psychoanalysis, 87:725-746.

Kalmanowitz, D. and Lloyd B. (2005), Art therapy and political violence, with art, without
illusion, Routlege. 21.

Kapitan L. (2010). Introduction to Art therapy Research. U.S.A: Routledge, Taylor & Francis Group.

Kaplan, S. (2008). Children in Genocid: extreme traumatization and affect regulation, The International Psychoanalysis Library. London.

Kestenberg, J., (1985). Child survivors of the Halocaust-40 years later. Journal of American Academy Child Psychiatry; 24:408-412.

Klingman, A. (2001). Stress reactions and adaptation of Israeli school-age children evacuated from homes during massive missile attacks. Stress, anxiety, and coping, 14, 1-14.

Klingman, A., Sagi, A., & Raviv, A. (1993). The effect of war on Israeli children. In L.A. Leavitt & N.A. Fox (eds.), The psychological effects of war and violence on children (pp.75-92).

Klingman, A., (1992). Stress reactions of Israeli youth during the gulf war: A quantitative study. Professional psychology: research and practice, 23, 521-527.

Knill, P., Barba, H. and Fuchs, M. (1995) Minstrels of soul: Intremodal Expressive Therapy, Toronto: Palmerston Press.

Kolb-Angelbeck, K. (2000). Winona speaks. In these times, 10, 12-13.

Krippner S., McIntyre T.M. (2003). The psychological impact of war trauma on civilians, an international perspective. Praeger, USA.

Manson, S. (1996). The wounded spirit: A cultural formulation of posttraumatic stress disorder. Culture,Medicine and Psychiatry, 20, 489-498.

McCann, I. L. & Pearlman, L. A. (1990). Vicarious traumatization: A framework for understanding the psychological effects of working with victims. Journal of Traumatic Stress, 3, 131-149.

McNamee, C.M. (2004). Using both sides of the brain: Experiences that integrate art and talk therapy though scribble drawings. Art Therapy: Journal of the American Art Therapy Association, 23(3), 136-142.

McNiff, S. (2009). Art- Based Research. London, Jessica Kingsley Publishers.

McNiff S. (2005), Art therapy and political violence, with art without illusion, Cited by

Kalmanowitz, D. and Lloyd B. (2005), Art therapy and political violence, with art, without illusion, Routlege. 21

McNiff, S. (2004) Art Heals: How Creativity Cures the Soul, Boston, MA: Shambhala.

McNiff, S. (1998) Trust the process: An Artist's Guide to letting Go, Boston, MA: Shambhala.

Melzak, S. (1992) 'Secrecy, privacy, survival, repressive regimes and growing up', Bulletin of Anna Freud Centre, 15: 205.

Milgram, S. (1964). Group pressure and action against a person. Journal of Abnormal and Social Psychology, 65, 137-143.

Miller P J, Wiley A R, Fung H D, Liang C-H, (1997). Personal storytelling as a medium of socialization in Chinese and American Families. Child De.elopment 68: 557±68

Muldoon, O., & Cairns, E. (1999). Children, young people, and war: Learning to cope. In E. Frydenberg (Ed.), Learning to cope: Developing as a person in complex societies (pp.

322-337). Oxford, UK: Oxford University Press.

Mustakas, C.E. (1990). Heuristic research, Design, methodology and applications. Newbury Park. Califirnia: Sage.

Nader, K.O. (1997). Childhood traumatic loss: The interaction of trauma and grief. In Webb N.B. (2003). Mass Trauma and Violence: Helping Families and Children Cope. The Guilford Press. New York London.

Nader, K. o., & Fairbanks, L.A. (1994). The suppression of re-experiencing: Impulse control and somatic symptoms in children following traumatic exposure. Anxiety, stress, and coping, 7, 229-239.

National Child Traumatic Stress Network, www.NCTSNet.org, Complex Trauma in Children and Adolescents.

Nevo, O. (1994). Troomat Hapsichologia Shel Hahumor Beisrael Bemilchememt Hamifratz [The psychological contribution of humor in Israel during the Gulf War]. Psychologia, 4, 41- 50. As cited in Silverman and Roberts.

Nietzsche, F. (1967 [1872]) the Birth of Tragedy and the Case of Wagner, trans. Kaufman, W.,

New York: Tanddom House.

North, C.S., Nion, S., Shariat, S., (1999). Psychiatric disorders among survivors of the Oklahoma City Bombing. Journal of the American Medical Association, 282, 755-762.

Nucho, A. (1987). The psychocybernetic model of art therapy. Springfield Charles C. Thomas Publisher.

Papadopoulos, R. K. (2000a) 'Factionalism and interethnic conflict: narratives in myth and politics', in singer, T. (ed) The vision thing: Myth, Politics and psyche in the world, London and New York: Routledge.

Parson, E.R. (1997). Posttraumatic child therapy (P-TCT). Journal of Interpersonal Violence, 12, 172-195.

Piaget, J., Inhelder, B., (1969). The Psychology of the Child: with a new forward by Kagan, J., translated from the French by Helen Weaver; Basic Books, Inc. New York.

Punamaki, R. (2000) 'Personal and family resources promoting resiliency among children suffering from military violence', in Willigen, L. Van (ed.) Health Hazards of Organized

Violence in Children, Volume 2: Coping and protective Factors, Utrecht: Pharos. Book

Punamaki, R.L. (1996). Can ideological commitment protect children psychosocial well-being in situations of political violence? Child Development, 67, 55-69.

Pynoos, R. (1990). Post traumatic stress disorder in children and adolescents. In B. Garfinkel, G. Carlson, & E. Weller (Eds.), Psychiatric disorders in children and adolescents.

Philadelphia: W. B. Saunders.

Qouta, S., Punamaki, R., El Sarraj E. (2005). Mother-child expression of psychological distress in war trauma. Clinical Child Psychology Psychiatry, 10, 135-156.

Raphael, B., & Wilson, J.P. (Eds). (1993). International handbook of traumatic stress syndromes. New York: Plenum Press. Cited in Silverman and Roberts 2002.

Razavi, Sh., (2006). Women's Claims for Equality in Iran. 1225 Islamic Politics, by Third World Quarterly, 27(7), 1223 – 1237.

Rosenthal, M., & Levy-Shiff, R. (1993). Threat of missile attacks in the Gulff War: Mother's perceptions of young children's reactions. American Journal of Orthopsychiatry, 63, 241- 254.

Rotter, J. B. (1942). Level of aspiration as a method of studying personality. II. Development and evaluation of a controlled method. Journal of Experimental Psychology, 31, 410-422.

Rynearson, E.K.(2006). Violent death: Resilience and intervention beyond the crisis. New York: Routledge.

Saigh, P.A., Green, B.L., Korol,M., (1996). The history and prevalence of posttraumatic stress disorder with special reference to children and adolescents. Journal of School Psychology, 34(2), 107-131.

Salmon, K., & Bryant, R. A. (2002). Posttraumatic stress disorder in children: The influence of developmental factors. Clinical Psychology Review, 22, 163–188.

Sandler; J. (1985) The analysis of defense: the Ego and the Mechanisms of Defense Revisited (with Anna Freud), New York: International University Press.

Selye, H. "Stress and disease". Science, Oct.7, 1955; 122: 625-631.

Scaer, R.C. (2007). The Body Bears The Burden: Trauma, Dissociation, and Disease. The Haworth Medical Press. N.Y.

Shehade, B., Rustum, L. (2003). The Idea of Woman under Fundamentalist Islam. Gainesville: University Press of Florida.

Shiang, J., Kjellander, C., Huang, K.,& Bogumill, S. (1998). Developing cultural competency in clinical practice: Treatment consideration for Chinese cultural groups in the United

States. Clinical psychology: Science and Practice, 5, 182-210.

Shields, J., Erdal, K., Skrinjaric, J., & Majic, G. (1999). Post-traumatic stress symptomatology among health care professionals in Croatia. American Journal of Orthopsychiatry, 64, 529-535.

Shilo-Cohen N. (1993), The Psychological effects of war and violence on children, edited by Leavitt, L. A., Fox, N.A. Lawrance Erlbaum associate inc. N.J.

Silove, D., & Ekblad, S. (2002). How well do refugees adapt after resettlement in Western countries? Acta Psychiatr Scand, 106(6), 401-402.

Solomon, Z. (1995). Coping with war induced stress. New York: Plenum Press.

Stone, D. (1998). Social Cognitive Theory. Retrieved April 23, 2007 from http://www.med.usf.edu/~kmbrown/Social_Cognitive_The ory_Overview.htm

Stouffer, S.A. (1949). The American soldiers: Adjustment during army life. Princeton, NJ: Princeton University Press.

Sue, S. (1999). Science, ethnicity and bias: where have we gone wrong? American psychologist, 54, 1070-1077.

Talwar, S. (2006). Accessing traumatic memory through art making: An art therapy trauma protocol (ATTP). The Arts in Psychotherapy 34 (2007) 22-35.

Terr, L.C. (1991). Childhood traumas: An outline and overview. American journal of psychiatry, 148(1), 10-20.

Thabet, A.A., Abu Tawahina, A., El Sarraj, E., Vostanis, p., (2008). Exposure to war trauma and PTSD among parents and children in the Gaza strip. European Child Adolescent Psychiatry. 17, 191-199.

Tucker, D. (2001). What's New About the New Terrorism and How Dangerous Is It?, Terrorism and Political Violence, 13, pp1–14

Uilmann, E., and Hilweg, Werner. (1999). Childhood and trauma, separation, abuse, war. Ashgate, Aldershot, Bookfield USA. Singapore, Sydney.

Van der Kolk, B. A. (2003). Frontiers in trauma treatment. Presented at the R. Cassidy Seminars, St. Louis, MO, 2004. Cited in Talwar (2006).

Van der Veer, G. (2000) 'Empowerment of traumatized refugees: a developmental approach of prevention and treatment', Torture, 10:-1.

Van der Kolk, B.A. (1996). The black hole of trauma. In Webb, N.B. (2003), Mass trauma and violence; Helping families and children cope. The Guilford Press. New York London.

Van der Kolk, B.A . (1987) Psychological Trauma, Washington, DC: American Psychiatric Press.

Van der Kolk, B. (1984). Post-traumatic stress disorder: Psychological and biological sequelae.

Washington, DC: American Psychiatric Press.

Volkan V. D. (2004). Chosen Trauma, The political ideology of entitlement and violence. Berlin, Germany.

Volkan, V. (2004). Blind trust. Charlottesville, VA: Pitchstone Publishing.

Volkan V. D. (2000). Transgenerational transmissions and chosen traumas: an element of large group identity. Group Analysis, 34: 79-97.

Webb, N.B. (2003). Mass Trauma and Violence: Helping Families and Children Cope. The Guilford Press. New York London.

Winnicott, D. W. (1984). Deprivation and Delinquency. London: Tavistock publications.

Wolmer L., Laor N., Gershon A., Mayes L., Cohen D. (2000). The mother- child dyad facing trauma: a developmental outlook. Journal Nerv Mental Disease, 188, 409-415.

Woodcock, J. (2001c) 'Trauma and spirituality', in spiers, T. (ed) Trauma: A Practitioner's

Guide to Counseling, London: Brunner-Routledge.

Yule, W., Perrin, S., & Smith, P. (2001). Traumatic events and post-traumatic stress disorder. In Silverman and Roberts.

Zahr, L. (1996). Effects of war on the behavior of Lebanese preschool children: influence of home environment and family functioning. American Journal orthopsychiatry, 66, 401-408.

Zeidner, M.(1992). Coping with disaster: The case of Israeli adolescents under threat of missile attack. Journal of youth and Adolescence, 22, 89-108.

DEFINITION OF TERMS

Hejab; an Islamic religious rule for women to cover themselves from head to toe, they only can expose the face and the hands.

Chosen trauma; a form of massive trauma which intergenerationally transmit, the shared mental representation of the historical traumatic event may evolve into what Volkna calls a "chosen trauma". The chosen trauma becomes a significant marker for the large-group identity

Transgenerational trauma (Volkan, 2004).

Complex trauma: the term complex trauma describes the dual problem of children's exposure to multiple traumatic events and the impact of this exposure on immediate and long-term outcomes (Cook et al., 2005).

Culture: the beliefs, values, behaviors, shared history, and language of a group of people at a particular time (Silverman L.G. & Roberts V. 2002)

Dissociation: dissociation, dissociation is an unconscious process that separates a group of cognitive process from the rest e.g. separates affects from cognition (Scaer, 2007).

Ethnicity: members of a group which share common background, geography, and physical characteristics (Shiang et al., 1998).

Fatwa: the religious authorization that sanctions massacres of a specific section of the population (Donnelly et al., 2004).

Fundamentalism: refers to any sector movement within a religion that emphasizes a rigid adherence to what it conceives of as the fundamental principles of its faith, usually resulting in a denouncement of alternative practices and interpretations.

https://www.igi-global.com/dictionary/

Heuristic research: From the Greek work heurisekin, meaning to discover or to find. Refers to a process of internal search through which one discovers the nature and meaning of experience and develops methods and procedures for further investigation and analysis (Moustakas, 1990).

Indwelling: Turning inward to seek a deeper, more extended comprehension (Moustakas, 1990).

Massacre: the killing of three or more people at one time in one area (Krippner, McIntyre, 2003).

Massive large-group trauma: Volkan 2004 explains that refer to the injury deliberately inflicted upon a large group by an enemy group.

Military community: Rynearson (2006) defines that military community are military bases provide housing and the work location for assigned personnel and their families.

Mourning: The process of grief; the feeling or showing in response to a lost.

Political Violence: war, terrorism and/or civil war and includes all the gross violations and aggressions related to this. (Kalmanowitz & Ll\oyd, 2005).

PTSD: as the psychological reaction to an event or events where both the following are present: 1) the person experienced, witnessed, or was confronted with an event or events that involved actual threat or threatened death or serious injury, or a threat to the physical integrity of self or other, 2) the person's response involved intense fear, helplessness, or horror (DSM IV 2000).

Trauma: being overwhelmed by helpless, hopeless feelings together with a whole mixture of undifferentiated emotions. The personality is temporarily put under immense stress and breaks down (Melzak, 1992).

War: war has been defined by Rynearson (2006) as a political act involving violence to achieve national objectives or protect natural interests.

Printed in the United States
By Bookmasters